LIFE
WITHOUT A
FATHER

Fathering
a Fatherless
Generation

Dr. Ansy Dessources

DEDICATION

Life Without A Father is dedicated to one of the greatest women in the world, Denise Gervilus, who took the risk to carry an unwanted baby. God gave her courage to go through it. She is now an active member at the Healing Center Community Church where her son Rev. Dr. Ansy Dessources is Pastor.

Dr. Ansy Dessources

CONTENTS

According to the U.S. Census Bureau,

24 million children in America

-one out of three-

live without their biological father in the home.

APPRECIATION & ACKNOWLEGMENTS

I thank the God Almighty who keeps me alive every day to fulfill my destiny. My beautiful wife, pastor Sherline Dessources, who has been doing a wonderful job in my life and with our three beautiful children: Sherlsy Anne, Jeremiah Ansy Junior, and Samuel. A special thanks to the Healing Center Community Church.

I also give thanks and acknowledgement to the following:
Marie Evelyne Jean
Bishop Shawn Patrick Williams
Carmita Charles
Betty Samedi
Esther Michel
Hedelle Jeremie
Mirsherline Pantophlet

Thank you to all of you!

FOREWORD

I am very gracious and honored to be asked to write the foreword for my spiritual son and friend's book about his life both before and after he became saved. He has given his life to the Lord. He enjoys his life, giving all of his spirit-filled energy to the Lord as his Lord and Savior. After traveling together with him on several gospel missions, I have personally witnessed his life demonstrating, that he is a Spirit-filled and loving shepherd for the season that we are now pressing our way through.

His book speaks of how God has always used His awesome power to transform the lives of hurting souls to become the most caring and nurturing pastors for their flock.

One of the things that are similar in both of our lives is that he mentioned in the book that he had a father that did not want him to enter the world from the time his mother conceived him into her womb and through later in life. I was born in the South and was one of those who never had the opportunity to lay eyes on my biological father. My very good stepfather raised me until I reached the mature age of ten. Then another chapter entered my life as my mother separated from him and migrated to the North.

In this book, I can truly relate personally as my life unfolded in many ways like his. The story he tells in this book is one of sadness, forgiveness and love. His book speaks of how God

5

has always used His awesome power to transform the lives of hurting souls to become the most caring and nurturing pastors for their flock.

When I think of Pastor Ansy's leadership, I am reminded in Jeremiah 3 where God said He would give us shepherds after His own heart and they would feed the sheep with knowledge and understanding. From the time he entered his mother's womb, God was molding him every step of the way for the life journey he would later be assigned to. God was preparing him to be a father to the fatherless in his charge as Pastor over the flock. He would have to learn and to teach about love in exchange for hatred inflicted on him by unloving parents.

Pastor Ansy believes, as I do, that the blessings and anointing of God should be embraced and adhered to with Godly intensions. He has demonstrated that the measure of earthly success is not based upon earthly possessions, but on the Godly legacy that one can leave in the lives of others. This book is and can be seen as a real-life guide for helping and giving directions to other leaders about caring for their hurting sheep.

Bishop Dr. Melvin Howard

PREFACE

Life Without A Father is a book based on the true events of several individuals sharing the pains, heartbrokenness, disappointments, and anger of their father's absence in their lives. For others, life with their father was a blessing, agonizing, magical, destructive, joyous, filled with love, hate, compassion, and perfect. Generally, a father can be in your life, while not necessarily comprehending what it means to be a father. *Life Without A Father* was inspired by my own personal life events of having a father in my life who did not want me or love me. I encountered abuse and devastation from him because he wanted my mother to abort me. His decision not to love me nearly destroyed mine and my brother's self-confidence. I made some irrational decisions in my life because I was desperately searching for his love and attention, but was constantly rejected.

I collaborated with five of my spiritual children in this project that grew up without fathers as well as others that had the privilege of having great fathers in their lives. I pray this book will change someone's life and strengthen their relationships with both their fathers and their children. Always communicate with your father. Let him know how you feel and how you would like him to do better because you love him. Regardless of what pain you may encounter in your father's presence or absence; always know that before you were born, your Heavenly Father, knew who you were and the person you were going to become. Fathers, your children are not mistakes; they are here by God's divine will. Embrace fatherhood. Build relationships with your children. They need you and you need them.

Marie E. Jean

INTRODUCTION

Family patterns are changing rapidly around the world. A rise in divorce has been accompanied by a corresponding decline in marriages. Moreover, the traditional link between marriage and childbearing has been weakened with an increase in the amount of children born out of wedlock, either in non-marital cohabitation or outside of the union altogether. These situations inevitably shift the roles of men and woman, not only in the relation to each other, it also applies to their children. These changes in family patterns signal a weaker commitment by parents to their children than those of previous generations.

Research reveals that 33 percent of children have no father.

-U.S. Census Bureau

Research reveals that 33 percent of children have no father because of one of these situations:

1. Some fathers lack responsibility because they do not know what their priorities are.

Some people have no idea of the meaning of responsibility. If you don't know what your priorities are there is no way you will ever be able to let go of the things that are not priorities.

Let's consider this example: If a father does not have a job, makes no effort to pursue a career, or accept any type of employment, how can he ensure that his child is cared for? It would be impossible. Today, when we look at young fathers, some lack responsibility because they have never had a father figure in their own lives. Because of this, they need to be taught to be a source for their own children.

2. They have no idea what a father is.

There are a number of men that sleep around with women without taking any precautions. All they think about is having a good time, giving no thought to the consequences. The minute one of these women tells him she is pregnant; he might say one of the following:

A) I am not ready to be a father.
B) We were just having fun.
C) Are you out of your mind?
D) You are on your own.
E) I just met you; you'll have to abort that thing.
F) I have no money, no job.
G) Look, I don't want to hear that. Get out of here and go look for the person who got you pregnant because it is not me.

A responsible man would say, I will do what I can to be here for you and the baby. I will let my family know about your pregnancy. Men have no idea of the number of women that have committed suicide because of the depression from having to face this responsibility all alone.

3. They are in prison.

Prisons all over the world are filled with men who created reasons to be there while leaving their children and spouses behind. God did not put a child inside of Eve for her to take care of that child by herself. God created Adam first in order to give him the responsibility of taking care of his wife and children. That was the deal, if I'm not mistaken. Some males have been in and out of prison. Do they care about their children or who is going to be the father figure in their life? Some children are forced to become part of a gang or end up getting raped or became rapists themselves. They end up quitting school and doing all kinds of negative things because no one is there to help them shape their lives.

4. They are on drugs or alcohol.

Drugs and alcohol destroy a lot of your brain cells. A man with brain damage cannot take care of their children when they become addicted to these substances. Some days they act like men and other days they act like wild beasts in how they treat their own children. Some children may start using drugs or drinking alcohol at a very early age and end up worse than their parents.

5. They were abused by a relative or other trusted adult.

Victims of abuse who become parents often don't know how to forgive the people who abused them, so they carry on in those patterns against whoever happens to be in their lives.

6. They have no maturity.

One mark of maturity is the ability to think before you make a decision and realize the effects of your actions. Consequences are an inevitable result of your actions. A prudent person is someone with maturity that refuses to fail on purpose, or by not being prudent but has a plan B in case plan A doesn't work. Life can take you straight to hell if you let it. This is the reason God gives you the key to control life when it is getting out of control, and your job is to straighten it in the proper direction. Some people never grow when it comes to maturity. They keep failing every day and have no idea how to redirect themselves in order to win in life.

7. They are lazy.

Young men and women are so lazy today with their bodies. All they want is pleasure, and they are not willing to work hard.

I chose the title *Life Without A Father* because my life was affected by the fact that my dad wasn't there for me as a father should be for a son. As a pastor, I have met so many people throughout my ministry and in the world with lots of defects and brokenness in their lives because fathers are not fulfilling their roles as sources.

Most people out there are doing wrong things because they never had a father's love or a father figure that could play the role of a father in their lives. When a child is raised without a father or father figure, it is hard for that young person to give or receive love. Young girls especially want to be loved, but when they cannot find love from mom and dad, they may put themselves in a position to be molested or abused sexually by some guy next door, a family friend, or some other relative. So many young people are spending a great deal of time crying on the inside. Some

As a pastor, I have met so many people throughout my ministry and in the world with lots of defect and brokenness in their life because of fathers.

masturbate a lot, some cut themselves, some are suicidal, some have terrible attitudes, and some behave poorly toward parents, teachers, or anyone that wants to bring correction. All of these things can happen because of this root issue of not having a father in their life.

I once worked with a Christian woman who divorced her husband for adultery. A daughter was born in the marriage prior to the divorce. After a while, she met a man that was in love with her and soon after they moved in together and got married. Her 14-year old daughter desperately needed a dad at home, not just a visiting dad in her life. She and her mother's husband developed a close relationship, but her mother had no idea what was going on. She thought it was just a father-daughter relationship. She later found out that her daughter was pregnant by her new husband. She was devastated. Apparently, the husband made sure he planned yearly vacations when his wife could not go with them. The woman's daughter explained to her mother that all the vacations they took every summer were to get away with her to have sex.

She became so angry at what happened; she took her daughter to a clinic and had her abort the baby. Since then her life as a Christian woman was never the same. The guilt of her daughter's abortion and the hurt of her husband betrayal led her to live a sinful life. When I tried telling her to get back on track as the Christian woman

As you are reading this book please remember to be part of the solution. Help children and young people who have no fathers. Help those who are desperate to have fathers in their lives or who are abused by their own fathers. Help those who become suicidal, full of hatred, full of anger, sexually active, and abuse themselves with drugs and alcohol. Know that God has a better plan for them and will eventually turn them into leaders who can change other people's lives from having to go through similar situations.

Today I, Dr. Ansy Dessources, am a prime example of someone who went through abuse and humiliation from my own father and in spite of this, I have been healed by God. God changed my life and enabled me to forgive as He forgives the whole world. Read and make a difference in the world. The Bible says, "You are the light of the world..." So go. Be enlightened. Light the world with His truth.

-Dr. Ansy Dessouces

1

LOST AND FOUND

"Linka, Linka, Linka," Grandma Yaya said in a song voice. Little two year old Linka giggled and started to dance as her grandmother sang her favorite song. "Linka, Linka, Linka." It was a memory that little Linka would never forget, a memory that would follow her even during the darkest places that life would take her in the future.

It was a sunny day in Dutch Philipsburg, Saint Maarten in 1993. A small Caribbean island located in the Netherlands Antilles, a person could drive from one end of the island to the other end in a single day. Palm trees lined the streets while highways and houses filled the beautiful mountains of the island which was surrounded by clear blue water.

In Sucker Gardens, Philipsburg sat a small shack that was no bigger than two master bedrooms together. Inside, twenty-one year old Mirline, her mother Felicia and father Thomas were sitting down in the living room having a conversation. They were having an in-depth conversation concerning the welfare of Mirline and her daughter Linka. Felicia and Thomas wanted them to move to the United States in order to avoid the hostile relationship between Mirline and Linka's father, Tony. Felicia and Thomas believed that Tony was abusing Mirline, and they feared Linka would be next; but Mirline insisted that despite how terrible their relationship was, Tony had never laid a hand on her or Linka.

A few weeks before, Mirline, Tony and little Linka were living together in a small apartment just up the road from Sucker Gardens. Mirline thought that she and Tony lived a pretty good life. They were devout Jehovah's Witnesses and went to church regularly. Both Tony and Mirline worked steady jobs and did their best to raise Linka together as a family. They grew up together in Sucker Gardens, and were next door neighbors. Soon after, a childhood friendship turned into puppy love and they became high school sweethearts. Mirline became a part of Tony's family and her parents did not like this since they were devout Christians. But Mirline was confident in her relationship with Tony and knew she wanted to spend her life with him, even more so after the birth of their child Linka.

One night after work, Mirline's sister Benite told her Tony was in their apartment with another woman. Mirline became filled with rage and anger. The two of them jumped into the car and sped off to the apartment. On their arrival, Mirline unlocked the front door and ran to the bedroom where she was shocked upon finding Tony in bed with another woman. The woman lurched to attack her and Mirline started screaming. When Benite heard the shriek she instinctively ran back to the car, reached in the back seat and retrieved a machete. She then ran back and handed it to Mirline so she could use it for protection.

"I'm going to kill you Tony and I'm going to kill her!" Mirline yelled, swinging the machete in the direction of Tony and the other woman. Heart pounding and eyes wild, Mirline wanted answers.

"Mirline stop! Stop! What are you doing? Stop!" Tony yelled, franticly, fearing for his life he could see this situation was serious.

With no clothes on the other woman ran out the side door and fled for her life. She never looked back.

Mirline turned to face Tony and began to yell obscenities while hitting him in the chest with her fists. The argument then escalated and spilled into the living room where Benite and Mirline both began yelling at Tony. They could not believe the level of infidelity they had just witnessed. Meanwhile. Tony was apologizing and trying to calm her down, but he would learn in later years that he made a mistake that would alter the course of his life forever. Mirline eventually grew tired from the argument and left Tony standing there as she drove off in the car with Benite. That had been the last straw for Mirline. She knew in her heart she would never reconcile with him again. Her heart was broken. She could no longer trust him and her happy home was shattered. Although he tried to apologize in the days to follow, Mirline would not hear of it. She had had enough and packed her things to move back in with her parents, along with Linka.

A few weeks later, Mirline was sitting down in the living room with her parents in a deep conversation. She was now a twenty-one year old single mother living at home with her parents. It was not what she imagined, and she wanted a change. Felicia and Thomas agreed to buy Mirline and Linka a pair of one-way tickets to America, and they would never return. During all this time, Mirline maintained a cordial relationship with Tony and allowed him to see Linka whenever he wanted to. However, she never told him she was planning to leave the country. If she had told him, surely he would have been devastated. His mother, Linka's Grandmother Yaya, would have been heartbroken as well and all of Tony's family would try to stop her, so she never spoke a word about her plans. Mirline was ready to start a new life, a life in the land of opportunity where she would no longer have to deal with heartaches.

In December of 1993, just a few weeks after Linka's third birthday, Mirline boarded a plane for New York City with Linka on her hip as they bid farewell to her parents and the only home they had ever known. Little Linka smiled and waved, unaware of what was going on. Her little mind did not realize she was leaving home and would not see her family again for almost thirteen years.

A few hours after their plane had taken off, Tony knocked on the front door of Felicia and Thomas's home.

"I am here to pick up Linka," Tony said.

"She no here, she go, she go with Mirline to America, she no come back!" Thomas replied.

Tony continued to ask questions in an attempt to find out exactly where she was going in America, but Thomas refused to tell him anything. Tony was devastated and could not believe it. He immediately went to the police station to file a charge against Mirline for kidnapping, but the officer told him that they could not do anything because they had no jurisdiction kidnapping someone to another country. The police station had no means to reach out to American law enforcement, especially with so little detail regarding where they were in America.

Defeated and hurt, Tony left the station and drove back to Sucker Garden to his mother's house. When news spread around the garden that Mirline had kidnapped Linka and fled to the United States the whole family came together. Tony, his seven brothers and his sister sat in chairs around their mother Yaya's bed and mourned the absence of Linka.

Grandma Yaya wailed with a deep groan from her soul that was so intense it was heard by the entire community. The whole house was in mourning. Her little Linka, who was born into her hands had disappeared. In an instant, every moment with Linka was now just a treasured memory. She would never get a chance to sing to her, laugh with her or just spend quality time with Linka again. For days Grandma Yaya and Tony mourned, and everyone sympathized with them. This family was known for always sticking together and being close, but when Linka left things were never the same. Everyone started falling apart. For a while they had hope that Linka would return, but when days turned to months, and months into years, they lost all hope of ever seeing Linka again.

Fresh Start

It was a cold and bitter day on December, 1993, in New York City when Mirline and Linka arrived in the United States. Growing up in a tropical climate, they were not prepared for the cold, harsh weather. As the brisk cold whipped across their faces it portended the harsh life they now faced in this new land called America.

Mirline had settled in Trenton, New Jersey with her uncle, his wife and their three children. Her plan was to find a job, save up enough money to move into her own place and provide for Linka as best she could. Her only motivation was a fresh start, which fueled her drive for success and her ability to support Linka.

Although the transition from Saint Maarten to the United States seemed to be relatively smooth for Mirline; it proved to be a lot more difficult for little Linka. When Linka began to see people she did not know and live in a home she was not familiar with, she reacted in the only way a young baby would. She cried bitterly for her dad and for Grandma Yaya and her cousin Anthony, but none of them were around to respond to her cries, causing her to cry harder. Linka was terrified; her world was forever changed before her tiny eyes. Just a few days before, she was laughing and dancing with Grandma Yaya, and now she found herself in a foreign environment surrounded by strangers. Linka could not speak English properly, so she could not even communicate her feelings to these strangers. Her plea could only be expressed through her cries and her pain could be seen in her tiny doe eyes. In her mother's arms was the only place she felt safe, the only place that felt a little like home. Would she ever see her father again? Would she ever return home? Would she remember anyone? Was anyone looking for her?

Early Years

By 1997, little Linka was gone and I was now affectionately known by my American family and friends as Mirsh, or Mimi. Leaving the island, my family and coming to America at such a young age had traumatized me so much that my brain went into defensive mode and suppressed my memories of that previous life. I had no recollection of that time or of any family members in Saint Maarten, but I always remembered my Grandmother Yaya's name, and continued to see her in my dreams at night.

Mirline and I eventually settled in southeastern Pennsylvania in a small community and lived in a cozy apartment. I had just started second grade at a new school, and I was excited to make new friends. School was not what I hoped it would be. On the first day I quickly noticed that I was not like the other kids. I was often teased and made fun of which caused me react by yelling and then crying. Nobody could read the signs that I was crying out for help and attention, instead they just thought I was a disobedient, rebellious child. It was very hard for me to make friends and I was often picked last in school group activities. Many students did not want a pudgy African-American girl on their team, especially one with an anger problem. I was the only child who was forced to dress myself, walk by myself to school, and do homework on my own. My mother's work hours forced her to be less of a mother and more of a provider.

Outside of school things seemed to be going great. Mirline had begun dating someone and he accepted me as well. I called him "dad" because he was around so much, but I did not seem to understand that he was not my biological father. One day he said to me, "I am not your father" and those words stuck with me forever. I was upset, hurt and I reacted by throwing things. I immediately began hating this man. It was like I had lost a father again. I never saw him in the same way and lost great respect for him; especially after it came to light that he was still married and had a child close to my age. Once his wife found out about his affair with my mother she began to harass us and even came to the apartment to threaten and fight with my mother. I still remember that day clearly. His wife was violent, yelling and using profanity while pushing and shoving my mother. There was no calming her down as she was clearly on a mission. As we drove away in the car, I sat in the back seat. My mom was in the front and his wife spat on the car window while yelling obscenities with her daughter right behind her. It was a moment that is forever etched in my mind.

Despite the embarrassment and confusion, my mother continued to date this man. His family had accepted me as their own, so I grew to become very close with his nieces and nephews who were my age. I even attended the same school as them. It was my experiences at this school that contributed to my becoming the teenager I would grow to be.

By 2002, I had started middle school at the local middle/senior high school and it was truly a different ballgame. These years were an experience that I was not prepared for. I consider it to be one of the worst years of my childhood. I always felt on edge and dealt with my nerves by playing with my earrings or my ear.

I attended this school for about a year and half and it was a sixth through twelfth grade school, so I immediately felt intimidated. The older girls were all taller and prettier, and many of them had nicer clothes. For the first time I was more aware of myself and my appearance. I felt ugly. I had braces and always wore braids and had the same yellow and grey jacket. I sometimes dressed like a tomboy and other times like a regular girl. I could not identify with myself and did not know who I was or what I wanted to be, so I tried very hard to be like the girls around me. I wished for expensive clothes and shoes like the other kids so I could be popular like they were. I never wore name brand clothes or shoes and never sported the latest hairstyle. Because of this I felt inferior. I was easily influenced by those around me. One girl in particular I seemed to look up to the most was a Hispanic girl. She had beautiful, long hair, new clothes every week and was popular. She received a lot of attention from the boys at school and almost every girl was her friend. It did not matter to me that she did not care about school and was even a bad example in a lot of ways; she was always giving me advice and being nice to me. Her kindness and friendship stuck with me for a long time and I never got to thank her. At that age, all I needed was for someone to talk to me, listen to me, understand me and give me positive feedback.

They did everything they could to destroy my confidence and self-image, and it worked.

Soon a clique of girls decided I was their enemy because of a particular boy. It was classic middle school drama. These girls were known for fighting and spreading nasty rumors.

They did everything they could to destroy my confidence and self-image, and it worked. I was soon fed up with them bumping into me, staring me down in hallways and spreading lies. One day a girl confronted me and we ended up fighting. I was suspended from school because I threw the first punch and had to do in-school suspension or risk being expelled. After that I had no friends. Everyone had turned on me because I had lost the fight. Even my own mother was disappointed in me. She called every single one of my family members and told them how I gotten into trouble at school. Perhaps if she knew what I was truly going through she would have reacted differently and been more sympathetic.

I had no role models in my life and no friends in school. I had teachers who were poorly trained at recognizing a troubled student and a mother who was working too hard to take notice of her destructive teen daughter. With no one paying attention and no one caring enough, the only direction I had left to go from here was downhill. When I moved away from here I would experience more things that would nearly put me in an early grave. This is my struggle, my testimony, and my life without a father.

A Cry For Help

In early 2004, my mother and I had moved again, this time to a bigger town closer to the city. By working so hard all of those years she was now able to purchase a home for us in a nice neighborhood with little to no crime - or so I thought. Every house had manicured lawns, newly paved driveways, and friendly neighbors. People were always outside walking their dogs and children played outside unsupervised. There was a nice park across the street along with a baseball field. It seemed like the perfect place to raise a child, but even good neighborhoods can harbor dark secrets.

After I settled in my new home I continued seventh grade at the local middle school and was fearless. When I started at this school I had already made up my mind that I did not care if I was a loner, and I was not into making friends. My experience at the previous school had scarred me; but gradually I began to make friends and begin to identify with a lot of the young teens there.

At this point I was thirteen and realized that I was a statistic. I was a young African American girl with no father and a barely present mother. I hung out with a group of girls and guys all the time and began to treat them like my family. We were all around the same age and all came from single parent homes. The one parent that we did have just seemed to overlook us. We all hung out consistently, looked out for one another and always helped each other out. We laughed together, cried together, got in trouble together, and even made stupid decisions together.

While in this group I acquired bad habits, such as staying out late, lying, cursing, drinking, and disrespecting my mother. We got into bad situations like underage driving, underage drinking, underage smoking, making acquaintances with drug dealers, gang members and street racers. We were street kids who were never home, instead eating dinner on the street, where we would get into fights. We were everywhere except home.

I grew to have more respect and honor for my friends than my mother for the simple fact that they were around me and my mother was not. I had no relationship or any type of friendship with my mother. She was gone by the time I woke up for school, and I was either still out or asleep by the time she came home from working a double shift. We never ate dinner at the table together, so I ate dinner from the local convenience store with my friends, or their mothers fed me. I did not see any reason to stay at home because my house did not feel like a home. There was no one there. It was just me all the time. My mother and I were always arguing and our communication skills were terrible. We were always hostile around each other, and after an argument I refused to speak to her for days.

A few months into the school year a puppy love friendship blossomed with another teen my age from the group. He paid attention to me and made me feel special, loved and important, although I knew nothing about these things. I had never felt this way before and I certainly wanted the emotions to continue. We could relate to each other so well because we were both products of single parent homes with absentee fathers. I had grown to have an unhealthy dependency on him and believed that I was in love. I wanted to be with him forever. However, our courtship was violent and even abusive. I thought this was acceptable because it was all I knew. But suddenly in eighth grade he rejected me and I had no clue why. It was the first heartbreak I ever experienced. I immediately began to act out. I was angry all the time and grew hateful.

I hated myself, my life, and everything around me. I wanted to leave and run away. When I told my mother what happened she just laughed. I can still remember that day like it was yesterday. We were sitting in the car parked at the doctor's office and she asked me what was wrong. I told her about his rejection of me and began crying because the pain was unreal. Rather than attempting to comfort me, she burst out with a hearty laughter. I was utterly shocked and could not believe my ears. I was amazed but disgusted at the same time. Though it was just puppy love and was bound to end in heartbreak, I was not expecting her to be so cold. Little Linka really died that day. I wiped my face dry, held my head up and never opened up to my mother again for years. In a sense I had been rejected by my mother. Instead of receiving a hug and hearing her say "these things happen and it will be okay," I got laughed at and mocked. My mother did not realize that the little girl in me was still yearning for her father, and that little girl was looking for love wherever she could find it. When she laughed, it was the little girl who heard it not the teenager!

By ninth grade I had bottled everything up inside and seldom spoke about anything. I would express myself to my friends but there was not much they could do. Pressure was building up inside of me. I loved going to school because it meant being away from home. I really hated myself. One night I went into the kitchen, grabbed a knife and began to slice my left arm. Tears filled my eyes as I cut and began to see blood. I just kept cutting until I felt pain and saw my arm covered in cuts. I bandaged myself and wore a hoodie for the rest of the year to cover up what I had done, but one day in PE when I raised my hands the gym teacher saw my arm and rushed me to the guidance office. I waited there until I saw my mother come in. The secretary referred us to a psychiatric facility at the local hospital and off we went. In the psychologist's office she asked me questions about my life and my thoughts. After our session she asked my mother about psychiatric medication. We left the woman's office and never went back. I never received counseling unless it was in school and we never spoke about it at home. Of course, I never recovered. It was just swept under the rug.

I had suicidal tendencies for years after that and consistently fantasized about what my death would be like. Eventually I tried again, but this time I tried a different method. I swallowed a whole bottle of pills one morning, threw the empty bottle in a drain and went to school. Homeroom came and I waited silently to die. Second period passed and nothing was happening. I went halfway through the day without experiencing so much as a seizure, no foaming at the mouth, not even a headache! I was shocked. I would later come to learn that God was with me that day and He had a plan for me that did not include a premature death. I was going to live whether I liked it or not. On that day I vowed I would still attempt suicide again, only this time I would be successful, but by His grace I never did.

Revisiting the Past

At fifteen years of age I started asking my mother a lot of questions about who my father was. I asked her what he looked like, what his personality was like, and most importantly, what had happened between them to cause her to leave him. Previously, whenever I asked why we left, she would just say it was because my father would have spoiled me if we had stayed with him, but I did not believe it. I needed to know for myself who my father was and reconcile with him. She realized it was time and that I was old enough to know the truth. She told me bits and pieces of her side, but also said that I needed to know my father's side as well.

In the beginning of July, in the summer of 2006, I was off to spend a month in Saint Maarten. No one knew I was coming except for my grandparents, Thomas and Felicia. The idea was to surprise my father. I was excited to see my grandparents and meet my father's side of the family because I did not remember any of them.

When I arrived, the first thing I noticed was the heat, the clear blue water and the friendly people! I felt like I was at home and my feelings were indescribable. I felt like I was right where I always should have been. My grandparents greeted me with hugs and kisses, and we drove off in the car from Princess Juliana Airport to Philipsburg. It had been thirteen years since the last time I was here! I found myself unable to contain my excitement and butterflies danced in my stomach. I was nervous to see my father and the rest of my family. I stared out of the car window looking at all the people walking on the street and feeling the ocean breeze on my face. I wondered, would they remember me? Would they accept me? Would they reject me? Would they feel resentment towards my mother and hold it against me? I was afraid to find out, but there was no turning back.

When we pulled into Sucker Gardens, my grandparents still lived in the same shack-like house across from my Grandma Yaya. Before I could even settle in, my grandmother Felicia immediately took me to see my Grandmother Yaya. We walked into her house, and as soon as I peeked into the bedroom there she was on the bed waiting for me. She greeted me with a huge smile and a hug. It was a defining moment, and we both cried. She looked the same as when we left many years ago. She looked just like she did in my dreams, with light skin and small round eyes. For the first time I felt warmth, comfort and genuine love. I did not want to leave. I was so comfortable just being by her side and being in her presence.

A few hours later a tall light-skinned, clean shaven man walked in. It was like looking into a mirror. He had the same smile as Yaya, and I knew instantly it was my dad. Although he smiled, he did not seem genuinely happy. I could not put my finger on what it was, but perhaps he was expecting a little two year old, not a developed fifteen year old. In Grandma Yaya's small house we sat and reminisced about when I was little. We laughed and laughed and laughed into the evening. Although the air was still heavy because of the past, in that moment they were happy to just reconcile with me.

One day my dad came to pick me up and we spent the day together. He told me everything that happened from his perspective and it was parallel to what my mother had said. We got some food and went for a walk on the boardwalk by the beach. My dad said he regretted his actions from the past and that if I wanted someone to blame then I should blame him, because everything that happened was his fault.

I learned that night that he waited years for my mother and me to come back but we never did. He found it very difficult to move on, but he eventually married and had another child. He had not told his wife until just recently that he had a child from a previous relationship, which explains why she was so cold to me when I first met her. It was evident that she did not want to get to know me, welcome me or even let me hold my little brother. My stepmom kept herself very isolated from the family and sometimes her eyes would speak louder than her words. Everyone could tell she was not handling my presence very well. I often wondered what would make my dad marry her. Despite his humble apology and assuming the blame for what occurred, I still did not know how I felt. I remained neutral but that would not last very long.

During my month long stay in Saint Maarten, I spent two weeks with Grandma Yaya. It was a memory I will always treasure. She was unable to travel much because her leg was amputated from a complication with diabetes; so our days consisted of long conversations, eating food, and watching reruns of *The Golden Girls*. We talked about politics, love, college, our family history, the family tree and what my life was like in America. The entire time Grandma Yaya was smiling she never looked sad or unhappy. She was always positive. Grandma Yaya expressed to me that she was afraid she was going to die without ever seeing me again. For thirteen years she lived with a broken heart, but now she was happy. I promised her I would return the next summer to see her again, but I would end up breaking that promise.

After visiting and traveling to all the different parts the island I was content in my heart. It was the last day and I was getting ready to leave. I had taken so many pictures and my dad had developed them, so I had to pass by his job to pick them up.

When I went into his office he sat me down and explained to me that he could not give me any of the pictures that I took of him or my brother. His wife had a problem with it and was afraid my mom would use voodoo on them. I did not even know what voodoo was and I tried to explain to him that we were Christians who went to church. Despite my pleas, he would hear nothing of it and feared that he would be in trouble with his wife. I said goodbye and left feeling sad. When I got into the car with my grandmother Felicia, I cried heavy tears. My tears continued for most of the flight back to the United States. I thought about how my little brother would probably never know me and how I would probably forget his face. It was clear that my dad picked his family over me and rejected me yet again.

This trip proved to be a pivotal turning point in my life. I went home a different teenager and realized that almost nothing in my life was what I thought it would be. I failed to maintain a relationship with my dad because of our last encounter, and he never seemed to want to maintain one with me. E-mails were not enough for me and I wanted him to try harder, but he did not seem to want to.

From that point on I realized that it would probably always just be me and my mother. We were all each other had and I resolved myself to never having a father figure. When I transferred to a Catholic high school, I became a better daughter and a better student. I gradually stopped hanging out with my old friends and doing bad things. I focused on school and just went through life. I respected my mom more and grew to be very thankful for her.

Two years later my mom had just came home from work and said she needed to talk to me about something serious. As I sat on the couch she explained to me that Grandma Yaya had passed away. Shocked at hearing the news, I did not want to believe it. Immediately I remembered the promise I made to her about coming to visit her again and I failed to do that. I never stopped to think that the next time I would go back home it would be to attend a funeral. I always thought I still had time with her. I immediately purchased a plane ticket and went home.

The funeral was devastating. There was not a single dry eye in the house and an ambulance was on standby because family members kept fainting and passing out. Everyone was hysterical and crying, I could not handle the wave of emotion that surrounded me. I just held onto my cousin the whole time and cried. We wished our big cousin, Anthony, was there to protect and comfort us. We were the three oldest of Yaya's grandchildren born into her arms. After the funeral it was like a big reunion only this one was held under the worst circumstances. I met cousins, as well as great aunts and uncles I never knew I had and was able to spend time with them as well. It would be the last time I ever saw them; the death of Grandma Yaya would split us apart even worse than the events from fifteen years ago.

I recall that I wanted to bring a camera with me but thought it was silly because I was going for a funeral. With the whole family there I now wished I would have brought one so I could have taken pictures with everybody. I asked my dad to buy me a camera and his words were, "Don't ever ask me to buy you anything because my wife will not accept it." Suddenly all the hate I felt towards him came back in a violent wave. I kept hoping for something that I would never receive, and that was a decent relationship with my father. I would eventually come to realize that while he and his wife tolerated me, they truly did not want me to be a part of their family.

I now knew who my family was and all my questions were answered, but I still lacked a father. I still lacked a relationship with him and resented his apathy toward me. When he missed one of the most important events of my life, my high school graduation, I was so hurt and upset. I never heard from him again and decided to move on with my life. I would later see how all of my decisions, relationships and morals were the side effects of the lack of father in my life.

Adulthood

Towards the end of high school I began to know God and tried my best to serve Him, but I ended up in a relationship with a man that compromised my faith and beliefs. This relationship also affected my home life with my mother and caused numerous arguments between the two of us. She had forbidden me from seeing him, and at the time I was rebellious. This relationship was an experience far beyond my years and something that I did not know how to handle.

During this time God was speaking to me about this terrible relationship, but I could not understand what he was trying to tell me. I was torn between my faith and really wanting someone to love me. Our relationship was terrible. Often I felt e he was treating me like a child. He had intercourse with other women to satisfy his flesh, but I refused his advances because of my commitment to God.

Eventually I broke it off with him and later entered into a relationship with a man who forced himself on me. At the time, I did not identify it as rape because we were an exclusive couple; but it was rape. After the ordeal, I felt cheap, disgusting and worthless. I felt like I sold myself to the devil at the expense of another person's flesh.

Not long after that I ended the relationship and started my first year of college. I went to school five days a week and drank every weekend. I used liquor to deal with the stress of school, the pain of emptiness, and thoughts of suicide. At this point I was writing poetry every day and read hundreds of books to escape from my reality. I loved reading about someone else's life because it took me away from mine. I often wished to be like the main characters whose lives ended in triumph. My life did not seem to be headed in that direction and it seemed like I was always being knocked down by a traumatic experience. I grew a deep hatred for men. I had no respect for them and could not ever see myself married or with children. I wanted to be alone for the rest of my life and did not ever want to experience pain again. I was tired. I was upset. I had been abused, raped, rejected, and mistreated. I was fed up, unhappy and everywhere I went people could see the pain behind my eyes. I was not myself. I wrote poems about death all the time and believed that death had to be better than life on earth. Poetry allowed me to balance my emotions and express myself freely. I had been so used to pain by this time that I began to get numb to it.

I had no reason to live and seemingly went through life because I was supposed to. I had no drive, no ambition and no willpower. There was no purpose in my life, and I was decaying inside. I could not hold a platonic relationship with men. It felt weird to be around them, and I would sometimes feel hostile. I very much hated my father and blamed him for everything I had gone through in life. I even blamed my mother at times because she made the decision to leave. I blamed him because he was not around and was not there to protect me. I could not forgive him and let it go. Both of their decisions altered the course of my life, and I went through things a young girl should never have to. I had never had anyone tell me I was special, beautiful or smart. No one ever told me the importance of self-esteem, the truth about love, how a woman should be treated or, more importantly how a woman should treat herself. I learned all this through my own experiences the hard way.

In my early twenties I started going to church more often, but I was not committed. I went because I felt like I had to or my mother would make me. However, I did believe in God but I was still a one-foot-in-and-one-foot-out believer. I had no understanding of Jesus Christ or the Bible. One day the Lord touched my life and I cried. I literally cried the whole day. I have not been the same since that day and I received the Lord Jesus Christ as my Savior. Through Him I met the Father. Though I still struggled with old habits, it would take a prophecy to change my life, and I could not believe that God could love me this much, or that I was worth blessing. He was the only Father I needed and the only Father who had been there for me my entire life. He was the Father that was with me when I was in my mother's womb. He was with me when I was crying to see Grandma Yaya. He was with me when I tried to commit suicide, and He was with me on my graduation day. He was with me when my grandmother passed away, and He was with me the day I started living for Him.

As young woman I had always been looking for love and validation from the people around me and I never got it. I was a broken young woman, and inside me there was a little girl crying desperately for someone to recognize her. Every time I saw a little girl with her father in public I would cry silent tears. I would be watching television and see a father and daughter interacting and I would get emotional. I was heartbroken and the older I got the more evident it was. I could not hide it. After I gave my life to Christ I realized that I could never move forward in anything that I wanted to do because I still had so much pain inside and never faced it. Though I have not seen my father for almost a decade and my search for him has yielded no results, I decided to forgive him. I pray for him and his family as well. I am glad I went through life without a father because I do not believe I would have had the opportunity to know my true Father. Though my birth father may not walk me down the aisle on my wedding day all is well because my Heavenly Father will walk me just as he walked with me my entire life.

Psalm 34:18 (CEB),"The Lord is close to the brokenhearted and saves those whose spirits are crushed".

To my mother, forgive me. I love you.

2

ABSENT FATHER

Being in the house as a dad doesn't mean that you are involved in your child's life. According to the definition of the word "dad" it means "source." A source is the main thing that gives life to all the branches so that everything connected to the branches finds life.

Not everyone has a good life just because their daddy is living in the house. Sometimes it's even more of a hellish situation. Living in the house doesn't mean that everything is great. People should know that a lot of negative things can happen. Many children are being molested or abused in different ways by their biological fathers, making it harder for them to trust anyone, especially those living in third world countries where people have no idea what is going on. Many of these nations have no laws to protect children or restrain parents from abusing their children.

Being in the house as a dad doesn't mean that you are in the child's life.

Some children are picked up by a father with a kiss and the child smiles with confidence, knowing that he or she is being protected by a loving father. Others are yanked by a dad with a mean face and they cry, knowing their life can be taken at any moment.

Young men women in America have been traumatized by many obstacles. I believe this is attributable to the fact that 70 out of 100 young people practice masturbation, sex, drugs, gangs, stealing and drinking alcohol. They feel unwanted and believe no one is there for them just to bring encouragement. They need people to say "It's okay. You'll do better next time", "I love you, you are the best, you're the best thing that ever happened to me, thank God, He gave me a son or a daughter like you, or you're going to be great in life". That's why so many young people have low self-esteem because they are never encouraged by their fathers.

Welcome to my Childhood Life

I was born on the morning of Wednesday, March 19, 1972. I became the fourth child out of seven. Prior to that year in 1971, the news came that my mother, Miss Denise, was pregnant. My dad, Mr. Jean, was mad. He decided to make a major decision to terminate the pregnancy. The fact is that he didn't want to have another child.

My mom objected to the idea of getting an abortion, but my dad threatened to abandon her with the baby. She realized her financial situation was not stable and she already had three other children in her care. For those reasons, she decided to make things easy on her and her three other children.

My mom explained everything to a friend of hers. The friend told her, "I can take you somewhere and they can help you get rid of the baby right before you blink your eyes." As they got to the clinic, they explained the whole situation to the doctor and he gave them a remedy that was supposed to turn the baby into nothing. My mom felt a relief just to be able to get rid of the child in her womb so her relationship with my dad could go well for the sake of the other three kids. She swallowed a pill for the remedy. Soon after that, she got really, really sick.

Her friend took her back to that doctor in order to find out what was going on, but the doctor found out that the baby was still alive! The pregnancy was still active. My mom was angry and asked "what do I do now?" The doctor replied to her, "Don't you worry. I have a better remedy for you. It will do the job quicker." My mom answered, "No! I really don't want the baby to get killed this time. Whatever it takes, I am keeping this baby. I don't care at all how Mr. Jean is going to react towards me and the baby." When she gave the news about keeping the baby to my dad, he said "I am not going to take care of that baby by any means." Throughout the pregnancy my dad never asked how she was doing and there was no excitement for my birth.

> My dad said, "I am not going to take care of that baby by any means."

Finally on March, 1972, in Port-au-Prince Haiti at Chancerelle Hospital, my mom gave birth to me. That day, after giving birth, my mom got sick. She couldn't even hold me for over three days. So I remained beside her. Through all this, my dad never came to visit my mother or me.

When my mom returned home from the hospital it was not a joyous occasion. It was the beginning of sorrow for me. My dad never held me and showed no pity whatsoever.

I was named Ansy. The name was given by my godmother and aunty. My dad hated me to the point that he wanted me dead. My mom kept the two girls and the boys outside of Port-au-Prince for them to live with the Dessources family in Crois-des-bourquet. After my mom and dad broke–up, I was treated like an animal. My siblings were now separated.

As a child, I was beaten for no reason, and was abused and humiliated bymy own biological father. He called me a pig so often I began to think I was one. He never sent me to school, but my grandmother, Genevieve the mother of Jean Dessources, felt terrible for us and sent us to a little church school across the street from where they used to live. I was nine years old when I first went to school. My dad was a sculptor who created wood art for a living. He used us boys to do all the hard work. We were beaten for any mistakes we made. We never received a proper meal and never had proper clothes to wear.

Sometimes we went to sleep without taking a shower; we slept on a mat and didn't even have a toothbrush to clean our teeth. People often called us monkeys. Our Aunt Bernadette didn't like the way we were treated, so she brought us back to the capitol of Haiti. For the first time I felt as if I was being treated like a human being. She was so kind to us that we couldn't believe it was true. One day she had to break the news to us that we were going back to our father. We cried bitterly. You would have thought we were going to be killed.

My dad called me a pig so much, in fact, I thought I was one.

After my aunt sent us back to our father, life became so hard for me and my brother Markenson. If I had the opportunity to kill myself, I would have taken it. Thank God it didn't happen. One day my father told us not to call him "father" and asked us to just call him "Jean." There was no way I would have called him that. I found a way not to call him, ever. My dad always found a reason to beat me up. When he couldn't find one, he created a reason.

When I turned fourteen, I started masturbating, sleeping with relatives, and stealing. I became an angry person, cruel and full of hatred. I could be at peace when my dad was away, but whenever I heard his voice or someone mentioned his name, it was just like my world shut down. I couldn't function when my dad was around and I had very low self-esteem. I thought I was inferior compared to everybody else.

My dad used to say "You will never be anything in your life." He loved to slap and kick me and even used a heavy stick to beat me.

My dad happened to be getting married at that time. My brother and I saw people getting ready for the wedding and they were all excited, however my brother and I weren't invited to the wedding. Cousins, uncles, aunties, and friends were getting dressed, making jokes, and laughing with each other. No one saw us, the two poor boys, watching everybody leaving because the entire neighborhood was invited. My brother and I just stayed all alone until we fell asleep.

One day, my uncle Toto had to travel to Port-au-Prince in order to speak to my mom about our situation. It was so critical that even my uncle Toto couldn't take it anymore. The reason he had made the trip was to plead with my mom to come and rescue us boys.

After uncle Toto had spoken to my mom, she went to Crois-des-bourquet to remove my brother and me from the miserable situation that we were in. My mom didn't have much, so she couldn't afford to have us live with her. Therefore she gave us to her mother to help raise us. My mom sent as much as she could every now and then as a contribution to help raise us. The school they sent us to wasn't a bad school, but the teacher often reminded us of our father by calling us "monkey" or "the two darker ugly people in the class." Sometimes the teacher would make us stand so that others could make fun of us by calling us mean names.

In the late 1980s, my mom moved to the United States. Soon after, I learned my dad moved to the United States the following year. With no supervision I was free to do whatever I wanted to do, so a friend of mine introduced me to voodoo and I liked it. I enjoyed its rituals and everything about it.

I was afraid of being around educated people because of my low self-esteem. I hated school so much, I decided to quit and become a sex addict. I was living a careless life, so I slept with many women to the point I thought I had AIDS. All of these behaviors were the result of my father who hated me. I almost destroyed myself because I did not know how to face him.

I was 21 years old when my brother Vaguy died. I dreamt that he was burning in the lake of fire; he said, "Give me another chance, I will change my life." The more he shouted, the bigger the fire became until I couldn't see him anymore. When I woke up, I heard a voice speaking to me about my life, saying I was living like hell.

The voice told me that if I didn't change my ways then Hell was where I would be going as well. That very week I gave my life to Christ.

I have overcome so many things in my life. I dedicated my life to Christ completely. I started reading the Bible, especially the New Testament. I read it so many times that I was able to understand the love of God for myself and the whole world. The biggest shock for me was when Jesus said ''Father forgive them for they don't know what they are doing." Jesus made that statement while He was bleeding on the cross with nails in His hands and His feet. Despite people making fun of Him, He still asked forgiveness for them. This was really an eye-opening experience for me on the subject of forgiveness.

I don't know your story. Yours might be worse than mine, but keep in mind that John 3:16 tells us, "For God so loved the world, that He gave His only begotten Son, that whosoever believes in Him shall not perish, but have eternal life."

Seven years later, my siblings and I moved to the United States to join our mother Denise. There was a challenge awaiting me, and that was to forgive my father. Hallelujah, praise the Lord God Almighty, it was the greatest thing God did for me before my father passed away. My dad was so shocked that he even told my mom he could not believe how I forgave him. My mom told him that I had Jesus in my life and that's why God made it easy for me. My father and I had an opportunity to hang out together before he died. He made me laugh with some of his jokes and he was the first person in the family to call me Pastor.

3

FATHER BY ACTION NOT BIRTH

A true father never walks away from his responsibility. It doesn't matter how a father started; rather, it is how he is going to finish by leaving an exceptional legacy on earth as a father. Women and children are affected negatively the most by those so-called fathers who love to have sex and populate the earth children without knowing how to handle their responsibility.

A Man Can Have Children But That Doesn't Make Him A Father

''You're nothing, you're ugly, your hair is too coarse, you're too dark to be my daughter.'' These were there words I grew up hearing from the man I was told was my father. Growing up it was the three of us girls. I was the older one. We all were raised by our great grandmother in Haiti while our mother was in the United States. My mother would travel back and forth from Haiti to the States. After I was born my mother traveled to Haiti with me so that my great grandma could raise me. She did this with all of her children. During her short time in Haiti she met a powerful man who had political influences. My mother became involved with this man and he moved in with us. I was only

> *A true father never walks away from his responsibility.*

one year old and my great grandma told me that the man was my father.

"Daddy please stop"…

"He's just drunk," great grandmother always said.

Why does he only pick on me? Why does he hate me so much? These are questions that a toddler shouldn't have to ask herself.

My great grandmother came from a generation where showing love and affection was unheard of. Yes, they loved their kids. However, they simply did not know how to show that love. This made it even harder for a young child to show love. I couldn't stand being home and when I got to be a little older, I started to go to my neighbor's and families' houses. I had this one particular neighbor who had a big white house. He didn't have a big family so he rented half of the house to many different people. The neighbor had two new renters. They were a middle-aged man and a middle-aged woman. The man was single and the woman had two children, an infant and a toddler.

I was very excited to meet my new neighbors. Little did I know that one of them would change my life forever. As I was in the front porch of my neighbor's house one day the new guy called me over to where he was standing. Thinking nothing of it I ran to him up to him. He led me back to his room.

"Wait, this is weird," I thought. "He's not allowed to touch me there." "This has to stay a secret," he says to me. It was late. I was confused and started to panic. I ran home to tell my dad what had happened. Instead of answers, I was met with a whipping for coming home so late. With the fear of another whipping, I shut up about what had happened between the neighbor and me. Now I was a confused kid who had been physically, mentally and sexually abused, and I had no one to talk to about it. I felt weird and my body seemed to like what had happened. I felt betrayed by my own body. Was it because I felt wanted and loved that my body responded that way? I couldn't tell. I was just a little kid.

At the age of ten I began to notice a man walking around the neighborhood talking to the neighbors, but he wouldn't come near our house. My mother's boyfriend left the house and said that he was leaving us. He had another family and he's going to be with them. I wondered if it was my fault. I thought I had driven him away. A few weeks after he left, the strange man who was walking around the neighborhood came back and this time he came knocking on our door. I watched from my bedroom window as my great grandmother talked with him with joy. With a big smile on her face she said to me "this is your father."

Wait, what? Daddy left us for another family remember?

The man scooped me up, hugged me real tight and cried. The man explained that he'd been trying to contact me for years but every time he'd tried the man who I thought was my real father would get in the way. However this time was different because he learned that the man had left. At that time I did not care about answering all the questions that flooded my mind. All I wanted was to stay in his arms because it felt safe.

49

Nothing could get me down from this feeling. He was free now to visit me, and he did so frequently. I visited him and his family. He had a wife and a one-year-old daughter. I also met his mother and father, my grandmother and grandfather. I was so happy that it seemed like a dream. To finally have a positive male figure in my life bought so much joy. I couldn't care about anything else. I was no longer left out. I had a father who loved me just like my little sisters did. The happiness didn't last long. My mother, who was in the United States the year before sent for my youngest sister and now she sent word to my great grandmother that she would like her to get my paperwork ready so that I could go to see her.

I didn't want to go. I didn't care if I stayed in Haiti, but at least I would be with my dad. He was my real dad. I didn't know why she wanted me now. She didn't want me ten years ago when she dropped me in Haiti for her grandmother to raise. Why now? I finally had a good thing going for me and she wanted to come and mess it up.

It didn't matter how much I cried and argued about it. I had no power to stop it. I traveled to the States to stay with my mother. She had a newborn at that time along with my other little sister who came the year before me. This made me at ease because it wasn't just me and her.

It was always my dream that when I turned eighteen I would get my father and his family a visa and we could all move in together to be one big happy family. This dream kept me going for four years. During that time my mother had a new boyfriend who moved in with us. My world broke to pieces when I learned that my father was murdered in Haiti.

I rebelled and my mother's boyfriend couldn't control me because I had no respect for him — or anyone for that matter. Now it hit me like a hammer in the face. Why did they lie to me about my father? Why did they tell me that a horrible man was my father for all these years? If only I had known him earlier then I would have known him more. Maybe I would have lived with him.

Although I didn't respect my mother's boyfriend, he was nice toward me. He respected my mother and provided for us. Whenever I would get in trouble, I knew that I could call him and he would bail me out. But he was too nice. At first, I thought that I was being paranoid, but he would give me these extra-long and tight hugs. He would say weird comments about my sex life with my boyfriend. He would kiss me on the lips. I never thought anything of it because he has a daughter about the same age as me and would do the same things to her. This made me think that it was a father/daughter relationship until my boyfriend pointed it out one day. "That's not a special father/daughter relationship. That's abuse," he told me. My boyfriend was concerned for my safety in the house. I was more concerned that he would tell someone and my sisters and I would be separated, so I ended the relationship with him.

I wouldn't even tell my own mother about what was happening because I simply didn't know where to start. I became hard on my mother's boyfriend and when it came to my little sisters I didn't play any games. I would threaten him with whatever object was around. A knife or chair, or whatever it was, I would use it. As long as it meant protecting my little sisters I would use it. Although it looked like I had it all together for a preteen, I couldn't handle it on the inside. I did not tell anyone. I started drinking and my mother's boyfriend was my supplier. I also started to smoke and later when I wasn't satisfied enough I started drugs.

I would manipulate my mother's boyfriend to buy my alcohol and cigarettes. I figured since he smoked and drank, I would pay for his if he would go to the store and buy them for me. Drinking opened the door to new friendships and with the friends came marijuana.

School was no better than home. I had many bullies and the school turned a blind eye to the situation. I decided since the school wasn't going to do anything I would fight. I wasn't afraid to fight of bullies.

I manipulated my mom's boyfriend to buy my alcohol and cigarettes, but drugs were hard to find. I had to make a different set of friends to feed my needs. Despite the teasing and always having to watch my back, middle school flew by. In an instant I went right to high school. My craving for drugs began at the same period of time that I started high school. High school was fun. I was developing body parts and the boys were checking me out.

It was during the second semester of my freshman year that it happened. One of the popular boys called me over to his side of the street one day after school. Thinking nothing of it, I walked with him as he led me to his apartment, which was in front of the school. As we flirted and played around, in no time the apartment was filled with a group of guys. I was trapped. One, two, three, four boys, honestly I lost count as I was just lying there, wishing I was dead. I wished that I could jump out the window but couldn't because of the white bars. Even though I wished for it, death didn't come. With a new found strength, I got up and ran out of the room. I pushed pass the group of guys that were still waiting for their turn. I ran all the way home hoping for comfort. At home, I was met with a beating for staying out late after school. With the fear of another beating, I shut up about the rape. By keeping everything inside I become angry, bitter, and mad at the world.

Going back to school was going to be a challenge. I had no one. Nothing could help me face it. I was alone. I recognized some of the guys who were at the apartment and they acted like they didn't know me. They showed no remorse for what they had done. I pretended nothing happened. I went back to my life by pushing the memories of molestations and rape as far as I could in my mind. Not being able to let out my emotions, I dove deeper into drugs and alcohol. I took pleasure in sleeping with married men. It made me feel pretty and special. I thought that being with an older man would bring protection and security. I didn't think of the harm I was doing to the families. I didn't care. I was all about me, my hurts and my feelings. At the same time, I was also hungry for the wild adventures that younger men brought. For this reason, I was never able to have a solid relationship. I was always going from one to another. I always felt like every man that I was with just wanted something from me. Whether their intentions were good or not, I would move to the next one before I found out. I went through the next semester drunk and high. On top of that, I saw myself very unattractive and become addictive to diet pills eventually weighing 130 lbs. In the beginning of the third semester, all of the students went down to the auditorium to take their class pictures. The school auditorium was really big and had two entrances. One was from inside of the school and the other was from the outside. The outside entrance lead to the main lobby. From the main lobby you could go through two sets of double doors that were next to each other to enter the auditorium, or you could either go up to the second level from the main lobby. The students were in the first level of the auditorium. No one was allowed in the main lobby or the second level.

A guy was calling me over to the main lobby and I recognized him. It was one of the guys that I bought weed from. He's cool, I thought, so I walked over. "I've got to show you something," he said. I was excited, thinking that I was about to get stoned, but he wanted to fool around. I wasn't in the mood. I already had my heart on the weed, but his mind was on something else. He forced me down to the floor as I tried to fight him off. I realized then that it was too late. His friends showed up. I can't remember what was going on in my mind, or even what I was wearing, but I do remember one guy that was there. His face never left my mind. He was wearing a white dress shirt, blue jeans, and very clean sneakers. I remember him especially because as I was surrounded and being raped over and over. I grabbed him by his nice white shirt. I pleaded with him to help me. He agreed he'd help me. My sense of relief left me fast, because in a moment he was on top of me.

To this day I have no idea how I got out of there. I do remember walking out of the main lobby door that led to the streets. From that day on, I hated school. I only went to keep up appearances for my mother. The only way that I was able to get through a day was by being high and drunk. Why would anybody believe me? I was better off dead I thought, but because I was raised in a catholic household, I believed if someone took their own life they would go to hell. I thought "Who would look after my little sisters?" I couldn't kill myself physically but I was dead inside. I became dark and emotionless, and filled with rage. Heavy Metal gave me a place to take all my anger out. It was another world- a world where everyone felt the same. It was the same rage, the same loss and the same self-worthlessness. Into this world, I was able to escape. I was able to do whatever I wanted without judgment.

One afternoon there was a knock on the door. It was my illegitimate father. Here was the guy my mother and great-grandmother said was my father but wasn't. He had a new girlfriend that lived in the same city as we did so he decided to visit. The new girlfriend really liked me, and asked me to move in with her, so I took them up on their offer. I know what you're thinking. Why would you move in with the guy that physically and mentally abused you?

Well, the lady had two sons that went to school and one of her female friends lived with them. They were all potheads and drunks. My fake father had no idea what was going on in the house. We were high every day. In the morning before brushing my teeth, I had to get high just so I could function. I couldn't spend a day without being high or drunk. If I didn't have the weed, I couldn't function properly. With the intention of using me to get free drinks in the clubs, my fake father's girlfriend took me clubbing with them. I didn't care that they were using me to get guys to buy them drinks because I liked the attention. I stayed with them throughout the last semester of school. Drinking, smoking, getting high and clubbing became a way of life for me.

At the beginning of the summer, I moved back in with my mother because she was getting sick. My mother was a voodoo priestess who struggled with wanting to serve God. She tried to go to church but it never lasted. She was married to this spirit and it would take more than going to church to get a divorce. In order to divorce a spirit, you have to lose yourself in God, in prayer and in service. My mother did not know that and she had no one to turn to. Every time she would try to go to church, a problem would arise and she would go back to the devil. This did not start with my mother. It started way before she was born. The spirit Jezebel claimed our family including all four of us girls. Specifically the spirit said that I was her daughter and I had to serve her when I became of age. This didn't flatter me because I saw how my mother's life was and I didn't want to be that way. Just because I refused to obey this spirit, it didn't mean that the spirit would leave me alone.

I found a part time job at a local grocery store. At the end of the summer my mother and I walked over to the school she wanted me to go back to. I didn't want to go back there but I still needed an education. The vice-principle told us that I didn't have any credits from my first year of high school and starting over was not an option because I was too old to go back to the 9th grade. I was 16 years old by then. My only options were to go to night school or get a GED. I signed up for the day school hoping that I could get the credits that I needed to go back to high school. I hated the day school. It was three hours away by public transportation. I started to go, but taking three buses a day was hard for me, so I would travel to the beach instead. I transferred to night school hoping that would be better.

Things were going great when out of nowhere my mother got worse. She became hospitalized. The doctors did not know what was wrong with her even though they ran a battery of tests. With my mother's boyfriend leaving, she had to be both the mother and father. Now that she was on her deathbed I had to pick up her role as the provider. I quit night school and became a full-time employee at the local supermarket. At the age of sixteen, I was the primary care-giver for my family.

With no one left for me to be angry with, I turned to God. Not that I knew Him, but I didn't care. I became so angry that I denied Him and became a Goth. I got sucked into Death Metal and Black Metal. Not long after my mother died, the landlord asked us to move out and she only gave us a week's notice. My sisters and I were close to being homeless when my first cousin, who I just met, from my mother's funeral asked me to move with her and her parents. Without no other options, my sisters and I moved 1,258 miles to my uncle's home.

At my uncle's house there was one important rule, "go to school." Little did I know that my cousin had already talked to a guidance counselor at the school and the counselor talked to the superintendent. I started high school at the age of 18. I was different from the other kids. I was older and a Goth. Rarely do you see a black Goth. A new state and a fresh start didn't stop me from hanging out with the wrong people. I meet a girl who practiced Wicca and in no time at all I was initiated. During the initiation, a dark force came over me and I passed out till morning. After joining the occult, drugs became more accessible. Witchcraft is not a game. Once you invite the devil in, it takes the power of God to drive him out and a divine relationship with God to keep him out.

Out of nowhere I became friends with this girl who I normally wouldn't talk to. For some reason I didn't like her. Maybe it was because she was always talking about her church. She would go on and on about how great her church was and that her uncle was the pastor. She had the same ethnic background as me so I tolerated her. During the second year of high school, my uncle's mother in-law came to stay with us from Haiti. She was a sweet old woman who demanded that we find her a church to go to or she would leave; so the family went church hunting. I didn't care because I worked on Sundays. However, during my off days, I would go with her just to keep her company.

Church was a new game to me. I would go down to the altar whenever the call was made. It was all fun and games to me. My uncle found a church that was closer to our house for his mother in-law to attend. The name of the church was The Haitian Ministry (which was later changed to Healing Center Community Church). She loved it. She asked all of us to go and visit but I was always working. Little did I know that the church was right in front of my job. The Sunday before Thanksgiving I had off, so I went to church with her. This was nothing new to me, but this church was different. I felt hot. I couldn't stand being in there any longer.

There was a fight inside of me during the whole service. I had no idea what the sermon was about and near the end the pastor made the altar call. My uncle's mother in-law, who I call grandma, looked at me and said, "Don't you think it's time for you to receive God into your life?" Without a response I got up and tried to make my way to the altar. The walk to the altar from my seat was long. It took all that I had to make it up there. When I finally got to the altar the pastor looked at me and told me everything that had been going on in my life and how the spirit Jezebel had claimed my life. No one knew about this- not my uncle or his family, not even my little sisters. How did he know?

Although I accepted Jesus as my personal Lord and Savior the fight was not over. The alcohol was still there, the lying, the sexual impurity, the stealing and the cheating. I was made whole through repentance but the rest was up to me. I had to be willing to fight for my freedom from sin.

My uncle became a father to me and his wife became like my mother. They became the parents that I never had. They gave me love and the protection that I craved. In the beginning, it was hard to accept them or even give them a chance. However, in spite of my stubbornness and rebellion the Holy Spirit remained by my side. God used my uncle and aunt as an instrument to turn my life towards the path that He wanted for me. I am so grateful that they allowed the Lord to use them to lead me in the right direction in my life. I am proud to call my uncle, my father, and his wife, my mother.

I graduated high school at the age of 20 going on 21. I got baptized and shortly thereafter I set out for college. In college, I felt alone. I didn't have the protection of my mom and dad or the church. I fell into the same old things. I spent three years fighting depression and alcoholism in college. I had reached my breaking point. After a night of heavy drinking, I woke up the next day in one of my friend's beds who happened to be a girl. I was so far gone that I turn to the same-sex relationships for love and comfort.

The Bible says in Matthew 12:43-45, "When an impure spirit comes out of a person, it goes through arid places seeking rest and does not find it. Then it says, 'I will return to the house I left.' When it arrives, it finds the house unoccupied, swept clean and put in order. Then it goes and takes with it seven other spirits more wicked than itself, and they go in and live there. And the final condition of that person is worse than the first."

In all of my messes and disobedience, God never turned His back on me. He wanted me. I didn't understand how a perfect God can want someone like me. Why did He love someone like me? Why me? It's simple. The Bible says in Jeremiah 1:5 "Before I formed you in the womb I knew you; before you were born I set you apart before." This means that God had a plan for my live way before I knew Him.

During Spring break, I went home, and as always, I attended service. In a clear voice I heard God say, "You insulted me." Tears burst out from my eyes and all I could do was cry. Who was I to insult God? I repented and surrendered my life to God without holding anything back.

I graduated college with a Bachelor in Social Work and was determined to help others people who have been in the same place as I have. Due to the lack of trust in men, my relationship with my uncle started to become rocky: however, with God's love I've learn to love him and not see him as one of those men who hurt me in the past.

It is not easy to walk in the path that God has for me. I trust that God will be there in everything that I do and He will steer me in the right direction. Through the Holy Spirit, all things are possible.

4

WHEN LOSING A GOOD FATHER

It makes a difference when you are experiencing life with a good father that is truly responsible. When they have a dedication to raise their children and do anything to protect and support them, there is a noticeable difference. Nevertheless, when the children really need a good father and the news comes that he died with maybe cancer, a heart attack, a stroke, or was killed in an a car accident, or something else, that can devastate you even to the point of committing suicide.

Sometimes people accuse God by believing that God allows them to go through the situation saying, "Why would you let that happen to me God?

Tragic news like that makes life seem to be fatal for you, because you don't know how you are going to recover from a tragedy like that. Many times in life things happen for a reason. You may not know the reason now, but certainly there is one. Sometimes people believe that God allows them to go through these situations saying, "Why would you let that happen to me God? Why have you taken my father away from me? Why should I serve you? Why should I go to church? Why should I even pray because I have no faith anymore? Why didn't you kill me instead of taking my precious father away from me? I want to die because my life is nothing now! Why me, why me, why me?"

They may ask millions of questions that make them doubt or lose faith. One thing we should know is that God always has an alternative for whatever happens to his children. God knows what we can bear. He will never put more on us then we can handle for our lives to be destroyed. A young lady lost her dad at a very young age. Prior to that her mother died when she was only 9 years old then 4 years later she lost her only father. The news broke her heart that day. To her it was the end of everything. Nothing could have made her think that God could have intervened on her behalf.

This is her story: I was the fifth child of my family. My father was considered a hero to us. He gave us everything we ever needed and was very supportive toward our mother. We were the apples of his eyes. He did everything to protect his children and his wife. He was a God-fearing man, a prayerful person, a covering for his household, an example for his family, and a great tool for his own church and our pastor. I personally was spoiled by my late father but I never knew God. I glorify God for giving me such a wonderful father. However, at the time I gave all the glory to my father instead of God.

The morning of July 4, 1999, my teacher called me and asked me to go to the principal's office. When I got there I saw my uncle and two of my cousins saying that they came to pick me up. Right there I felt like something must have been wrong and I asked my uncle "What is wrong?" My uncle started crying and said, "Your father has died in a severe car accident this morning." To me it felt life my life had ended because my friend and hero was gone. I wanted to poison myself or do some strange things to end my life. I stopped going to church. I didn't believe in God anymore and I had nothing to do with faith at all.

One day after a long while, I was watching television with my family when tele-evangelist, Reverend Billy Graham, came on with a message I had never heard before. Rev. Graham quoted a portion in the book of Mark.

Mark 8:34-37, "And he summoned the crowd with his disciples, and said to then, if anyone wishes to come after Me, He must deny himself, and take up his cross and follow Me. For whoever wishes to save his life will lose it, but whoever loses his life for My sake and the gospel's will save it. For what does it profit a man to gain the whole world and loses his soul? Or what can you give in exchange for your soul?"

I was never concerned about my soul before because everything was fine but my soul wasn't saved. I used to go to church with my late father and it was an incredible relationship. I didn't have to pray or acknowledge my sins, but now Rev. Graham showed me that I was living in sin and even worse, if Jesus came back right now where was my soul going to be? What if something happens today? Anything can happen at any moment. Before his death we were joking around telling each other how much we loved each other, but I didn't know what was going to happen just two or three hours later.

We cannot guarantee tomorrow but Jesus is the center of it all. Jesus holds tomorrow and our future. That night, for the first time in my life, I was concerned about my soul. That moment I gave my life to Jesus and my life is different. Today, through Christ I really know how to handle situations and how to remain steady because everything happens for a reason.

5

FATHER, WHERE ARE YOU?

Daddy, where are you? Why did you decide to leave me? I need you. Mommy left, and now you. Why did you leave me in the hands of strangers? Don't you love me? Why are you not looking for me? Tears..........I need you daddy, please come and rescue me. These are the words I used to hum in distress when I realized how much I needed my daddy. I was looking for him. Every time I would see a man who looked like him, I thought he was my daddy. I could not understand why he decided to abandon me when my mother left for the United States.

Growing up without my parents was a time that was not only burdensome, but incomprehensible. I was young; I did not understand why my mom had left me for my grandmother to raise. Sixteen years later after my mom and I reunited, she told me everything.

My mother was pregnant with me when she was 19 years old and still in high school. In Haiti, the classes continue beyond the 12th grades as opposed to the U.S. During that time; my father was a good supportive boyfriend throughout the whole pregnancy. Surprisingly, he was still there after I was born, and continued being a good father. When I turned two years old, my mother had to leave Haiti to come to the United States. As soon as my mother left, my father disappeared.

I was now left with my beautiful grandmother, and of course; she spoiled me. Although she gave me everything I needed, love and affection, I still had a void in my life. My grandmother was a religious woman. She attended every church service, bible study, and anything that was going on in the church. She accompanied me to every event, and activities that was going on there. She did her best to keep my mind occupied because I was still missing both my mom and my dad.

A relative that often came to visit my grandmother and I did the worst thing that I could have imagined in my life. I was 10 years old when he did the unthinkable. Wait a minute; this is my uncle, why is he touching me like that? I don't' think that is right. Oh no, what are you doing? Stop touching me. Finally, he forced himself on me. I said stop, stop, it hurts stop…and he covered my mouth and raped me. I cried bitterly for my mom and dad. I could not tell my grandmother what happened. I was ashamed. I thought it was my fault. My innocence was violated and as I got a little bit older that changed my viewpoint toward men completely.

Another sad day, my mom left, my dad left, and now my grandmother was leaving me too. When will people stop abandoning me? When my grandmother left, I will be all alone. I was now 13 years old when my grandmother left for the U.S. Prior to her leaving, she made arrangements for me to go to boarding school. That was the beginning of my path to destruction. My grandmother thought she did me a favor by sending me to boarding school; instead it made my life miserable. I had no self-esteem or confidence because I felt unwanted.

The first few months there, I cried inconsolably because I was missing my grandmother. In my mind, I thought nobody loved me. So I began to think about my father regularly, asking why he did this to me. I cried in a loud voice and said, you were not there, my uncle raped me, and it hurt so much. I wanted to run to you, but I could not find you. I wanted to feel safe, love, but you were not there. At that time, I actually felt I was an orphan.

I spent three years in boarding school. Afterwards, I did not have a home to go to because my grandmother did not trust my relatives. I am not sure if she knew or felt something happened to me, so she asked one her friend who was a nun if I could stay with her. When I got there, everyone welcomed me with open arms. There were six other girls living in the house. I was comfortable and happy because I had a few of the girls that were my age. My mom and my grandmother both send money to them on a regular basis so I can be cared for.

After a few months, things begin to change. People in the house started to act strangely toward me. They would curse me out for no reason; make up lies about me, and just talk about me to destroy my character. One day I overheard everything that they were saying about me, they were even planning to kick me out of their house. Their behavior and attitude affected me so badly, I told myself, I had enough. I am just going to kill myself and get it over with. My mom, my grandmother, and my dad are not in my life, so I had no reason to live anymore.

Immediately, I went to the bathroom and poured some Clorox in a cup, and I closed my eyes and prepared to drink it. As I was about to open my mouth to drink the Clorox, my friend walked in the bathroom and said what are you doing? I froze and could not say anything. She smelled the Clorox and took the cup away from me and asked again what are you doing? Are you trying to kill yourself? Why would you do that? She then took me by the hand, and we went inside the room. By now, everyone in the house was aware of what I had tried to do. They began to make fun of me, laughing at me, showing no sympathy. I blamed my father for not being there for me. If my father were in my life, I would not have gone through all of these tribulations.

I want to tell you, when God has a plan for your life, no one can change it. It was God that sent my friend to the bathroom to take away the cup. A few days after my suicide attempt, my mother called me and had my step-father's brother picked me up to stay with him temporarily while they got the paperwork ready to come to the United States. I could not contain myself. I was just happy and could not wait to see my mom and grandmother. After 16 years of pain and sorrow, I was finally reunited with my mother.

This is how someone's life can be destroyed. It began with my mother leaving and my father abandoning me. As much as I needed my mom, I needed my dad even more. I wanted to feel his warmth and the comfort of his love. My life did not have to be the way it was. My father's absence affected me greatly, but I am thankful to be alive. All this time I spent thinking about my earthly father, and all along my Heavenly father was there for me, and all I needed was Him. I had to learn to let go and invite Jesus Christ into my life as my lord and savior. The power of forgiveness is wonderful. Once I forgave my father, I was free from all the pain.

To God be The Glory.

6

WHEN DADDY IS A STRANGER

My father and I were never close. There were times I thought I knew him, but I guess I never truly knew him because he was always a stranger. I never knew what my father expected of me because I didn't know him that well. My father was my mother's first love. It was a forbidden love because my father was what we call today a "player." My mother had to end the relationship because of his lack of faithfulness and commitment.

My mother was a good-hearted woman, with a desire to serve others and help youngsters. She was a genius in math and a woman with character. She had a dream to become a designer and a nurse, but her dreams were crushed when she decided to leave school. She believed in education and that it was a necessity to succeed in life, but she had to make a sacrifice to use the money she saved for her schooling to take care of her little sister. My mother was very hopeful; she believed that once someone's mind is set to fulfill the task, it had to be done.

A couple of years later, she met her husband. Together, they conceived five children and miscarried four. After years of marriage, my mother divorced. My mother and father would meet again years later and rekindle their love. After having five children, my father decided he didn't want to have any more kids because of his age. My mother also agreed because she was already in her forties. But God had another plan. Suddenly, my mother found out she was pregnant with a little girl. It wasn't good news for them, but it was something that couldn't be undone. Probably in their minds it happened by accident, but for God it was just the beginning of a new plan.

My mom was afraid she might have lost this baby because she was sick throughout the whole pregnancy. My mother was going through this alone while having to take care of her other children because my dad was now living in the United States. My mom spent the whole nine months of pregnancy going back and forth to the doctor; sometimes they kept her for more than a week for observations. After a visit to the doctor's office, my mother returned home sad. Her children asked her, "Are you ok mommy? What happened? Is everything ok?" She sadly replied "the doctors couldn't stop apologizing because after performing some tests, the doctor believed he had poked the baby's eye. After this incident, she thought the baby had died because she never felt it moving in her stomach.

Two months after the incident, my mom was experiencing severe abdominal pain. She was rushed to the hospital, and the doctors suggested the best thing for her to do was to take the baby out as soon as possible because the baby might have died. Amazingly, the baby was alive. My mother was unconscious and not aware that the child had lived. Once she became conscious, they brought the baby to her, and she was surprised and happy. This is how I came into the world.

Growing up I didn't know much about my dad. The only thing I knew was that he was living in the United States and working at Princeton University. My father was not a good provider. Instead of sending money to take care of his children, he chose to squander his money on women. I know my mother knew of his doings because I remember some of the arguments that used to occur every time he came to visit us in Haiti. I was small and did not remember the purpose or a particular reason for the arguments, but one thing I do remember is that I was always the one to blame.

One of the arguments that I remember clearly as if it happened yesterday occurred when my mother found out that my father was having an affair with my late uncle's wife. My mom was very mad at him, and I remember my dad standing in the middle of the street speaking in a loud voice, saying he was not my father. He told my mom that he did not want me anymore. I was standing there, not having a clue of what was going on. That was the last memory I had of my dad until my mother passed away.

I was nine years old when my mom died. I remember growing up with hatred in my heart, not necessarily toward my dad, but men in general. When my mom died, my father never called to find out how I was coping with my mother's death. After she died, I felt lonely because I missed her terribly. When I turned fifteen, I began to develop hatred for my father because of how he treated my mother.

My past is a story that I can only now begin to understand. My life can bring happiness, but also be a nightmare that could transform me forever. My life had been nothing but a rocky mountain that I kept on climbing. Losing a mother at nine is a pain without end. Three years later, I was separated from the ones who raised me, and forced to go live with a father that I had painful memories of. I was scared to live with him, but I was also excited because I always wanted to experience his parental love.

I wanted to know the real him. I tried to let go of some of those grudges I had toward him. I arrived in the United States on July 31, 2008, not knowing what to expect from him. He did not know me that well, and I did not know him. I had so many questions about how life was going to be. Would he be able to love me for who I am? Did he really mean what he said about me not being his daughter those many years ago? I decided to just let it be. It was okay living in the house because he was never around. At times, I would stay in the house alone because he was working. I was happy to know he was coming home at the end of the day. I felt secure even though he wasn't present physically. I used to cook for him, do his laundry and clean his room. Surprisingly, I had a great time with him, and I felt loved by him for the first time in my life. What happened in the past never once came to my mind.

Unfortunately, the love I thought he had for me was gone. After two weeks of living with him, he wanted me to move out and live with people that would be able to help me. "What does that mean?" I wondered. He explained that because of his language barrier, he would rather I live with someone who is already comfortable with the Haitian language. I told him that I would do whatever it takes to adapt quickly to the language. I wanted to experience living with him, but he had already made up his mind.

I moved to another city and was going to school. It was the beginning of a whole new life for me. Life started to be hard for me, and the first person that usually comes to my mind to blame was my father. I didn't blame him for the things that were happening in my life, but instead I blamed him because he felt powerless in the situations. I used to talk to him about everything that was going on, how I cried day and night because I was unhappy, but he never did anything about it. What was it about me that he did not want? What was he running away from? Is it responsibility? What did I do? I started to think that everything was my fault.

I was sad all the time and did know how to comfort myself, so I got a boyfriend. He was everything I needed because he showed me that he cared about me. I had no idea if he was just pretending to care or not, but at this point I didn't' care because all I needed was someone to talk to. He was always there, always available to wipe away my tears, to let me cry on his shoulders, to hold me tight in his arms, and show me that he cared.

I was young, naïve and stupid, and eventually developed a prideful spirit. I began to develop some discomfort at receiving help from my father, even if I needed it. There was no reason for him to try to help me now financially. I wanted to let him know that a father doesn't just take care of his daughter with money, but love and affection. And for the first time I was taking money from a man, my boyfriend. That same year, I lost my father on a trip that he took to celebrate his sixtieth birthday. I can remember every second of that day. I received news right after I got out of the shower, and remember putting some clothes on seven hours later because I had no strength to stand or do anything else. I traveled for the funeral, and when I came back, I started going to church and began to get involved in the church and ended my relationship with my boyfriend. I decided that I would change my life.

From time to time, I think about my dad and how those two weeks we spent together were the greatest moments of my life. He loved to dance; sometimes we would just dance to the beats of our hearts in the middle of the kitchen. Maybe if he were still alive my life would have been different. It was hard to let go of the blames and grudges that I had against him.

I was working hard in school to the point where every semester I was on the honor roll and at the end of the year I received an academic award. These things meant nothing to me because nobody was ever there to support me, or even go to the ceremonies. I had no dreams. I didn't know who I was and why I was put on this earth. I was lost, hopeless and felt I was worthless and had no purpose. I remember once having a dream where I would take care of my mother and my siblings. I saw how she struggled to care for us, and I wanted to do the same for her. I told her once "mom, I don't care about what I become in life, I just want to have enough money to take care of you." I still remember the smile that she had on her face after hearing that statement. But that dream died when God took her.

After the first week living with my dad, I told him that I would love to take care of him when I grow up "I will already be in my grave," he replied. His declaration has come to pass. All I ever wanted was to receive some parental love, and my dad had the last opportunity to allow me to experience it, but he refused to do so. I believed that by living with a parent I would be comfortable and happy, and that it would definitely take away the feeling of sadness that I feel when family and friends talk in glowing terms about their parents.

My mother used to tell me that God was a grown man who did whatever He wanted, whenever He wanted. So I started to engage in masturbation because I thought that was my only way to happiness and the only way to feel good about myself. When I was having trouble sleeping, I masturbated myself to sleep, and that was my life. There was always a sense of guilt that followed and I experienced depression every day. It didn't help me to achieve anything helpful for my life. The guilt that I usually felt was an indication that it was wrong to do. I tried to quit multiple times, but I couldn't. It bothered me to the point where I took the courage to talk to a lady in the church I used to worship at about it. She explained to me that she also struggled with masturbation, and I just had to pray about it. I replied ok, but did it work? No, it did not.

I decide to attend another church, and the spirit of the Lord used the pastor mightily to speak to me about my life. He was able, with the help of the Holy Spirit of course, to tell me everything that I had ever done in my life.

He even explained to me the sorrows and pain that I experienced. But most importantly he introduced me to a four letter word, HOPE. The word hope is very powerful, since then, it became my motive. He helped me overcome masturbation. He explained to me the power and authority that I had over sin and temptations. He confessed that he was not holy and urged me not to see him as someone who never sinned or as a person who had never been through stuff; and that was my green light to opening up to him. He encouraged me to pray more, because when I pray the devil gets mad and that's why he comes in my dreams to attack. It is good when the enemy attacks because it means that you are not his. The enemy would never attack the ones that are his, if he did; the kingdom would be divided. Not only did he spend a lot of time counseling me, but he showed me that he trusted me, he believed in me and if I fall, he falls. This has helped me to keep on climbing my rocky mountain. The only difference is this time I'm climbing it with faith and hope. This man is not only my pastor; he is my father and most importantly my best friend. Having a dad in your life means a lot, a dad is there to fulfill the task and make sure that it is done. The fear that I have for this man is what keeps me going. Sometimes I want to give up, but I remember that there's someone who counts on me and that it will destroy him if I fail in life. People find me crazy when I say this: "if my parents wouldn't have died, I wouldn't be who I am and where I am today."

I've turned out to become a quiet, different and interesting young girl. I'm very quiet because I listen twice as much as I speak. After all, that is the whole purpose of having two ears and only one mouth. But now, once I finally open that mouth to say something, it has to be something that people can learn from, and that can impact them in certain ways. People are fascinated by the hope that I have today.

Growing up, I've always had a fear of trusting and getting close to people and I thought this fear was the result of my losing people that were close to me. That was my mindset. I thought that once I got close to someone, I had to lose that person because that's how it had been all my life. I even started to think that it was my fault; I was "bad luck" to people. That's why I always kept to myself, not because I wanted to be anti-social.

These experiences at an early age led me to pulling away, and not trusting people. With hope, these thoughts changed. Because I realized that hopeless people can't move on, they are stuck in a box, just like I was, and all they will be doing is crying like a baby like I used to do, and blaming others for what they have done to them, just like I was doing to my dad, watching their lives pass by. It's true that my past was hard, but I don't tell people about it to pity me, because my past does not determine my future. It was a nightmare, but now it becomes a pleasant dream that brings not only happiness but joy and hope. How? Well, because a new person was born from it; an individual with a desire to help those with no hope. An individual with a desire to help orphans and young people to climb this mountain called life. There are a lot of others like me; the only difference is they have no hope. My past gave birth to the new me; it shaped me, to become who I am. Through God's love and my daddy's love, I forgave my father for all of his past mistakes. I believed that all of these things were meant to happen that way in order to meet God honestly and be in communion with him and my wonderful daddy that I have now.

Being in situations like mine is hard, but it's harder to have hope for your trials. Most people don't achieve their goals because they give up too soon. They quit after they get knocked down a few times. When what seems impossible comes my way, I think about all the times I made it through yesterday. I know if I just hold onto God, my dreams, and persist, then I'll reach my destiny sooner or later. One more thing that I had to let go of was the saying that the sky is the limit, I've come to realize that I have no limit in fact, the sky is my main floor leading me to my destiny.

7

WHAT IS A TRUE FATHER?

The Greek word for father is "source." A source is something that provides a need for something or someone. A source never stops providing because that is the essence of its nature. It is impossible for a source to cease giving the substance that is in it unless it is merely a branch that was once connected to a source, but is now unable to provide because it has been disconnected. God is the perfect example that fathers need to follow so that they can be a source for their children. God is the source for the entire world. As a matter of fact, God never stops providing for His children. That is why one of His names is Jehovah-Jireh meaning, "the one who provides."

The Bible is a Perfect Example

Genesis 1:1-31 reads, "In the beginning God created the heavens and the earth. Now the earth was formless and empty, darkness was over the surface of the deep, and spirit of God was hovering over the waters. And God said, let there be light, and there was light. God saw that the light was good, and He separated the light from darkness. God called the light day, and the darkness He called night. And there was evening and there was morning—the first day. And God said, let there be an expanse between the waters to

> *God never stops providing for His children that is why One of His names is Jehovah-Jireh.*

separate the water from the water. So God made the expanse and separate the water the water under the expanse from the water above and it. And it was so. God called the expanse sky. And there was evening and there was morning- the second day. And God said, let the water under the sky be gathered to one place, and let dry ground appear. And it was so. God called the dry ground land, and the gathered waters he called seas. And God saw that it was good. Then God said, let the land produce vegetation: seed-bearing plants and the trees on the land that bear fruits in it, according to their various kinds. And it was so. The land produced vegetation: plants bearing seed according to their kinds and trees bearing fruit seed in it according to their kinds. And God saw that it was good. And there was an evening and there was morning, the third day. And God said, let there be lights in the expanse to the sky to separate the day from the night, and let them serve as signs to mark seasons the days and the years. And let them be lights in the expanse of the sky to give light on the earth. And it was so. God made two great lights—the greater light to govern the day and the lesser light to govern the night. He also made the stars. God set them in the expanse of the sky to give light on the earth. To govern the day and the night, and to separate the light from darkness. And God saw that it was good. And there was evening, and there was morning—the fourth day. And God said, the water teem with living creatures, and let birds fly above the earth across the expanse of the sky. So God created the great creatures of the Sea and every living moving thing with which the water teems, according to their kinds, and winged bird according to its kinds. And God saw it was good. God blessed them and said. Be fruitful and increase in number and fill the water in the sea, and let the birds increase on the earth. And there was an evening, and there was morning—the fifth day. And God said, let the land produce living creatures according to their kinds: livestock, creatures that move along the ground, and wild animals, each according to its kinds. And it was so. God made wild animals according to their kinds, the livestock according to their kinds, and all the creatures that move along the ground according to their kinds. And God saw it was good. Then God said, let us make man in our image, in our likeness, and let them rule over the fish of the sea and the birds of the air, over livestock, overall the earth, and over all creatures that move along the ground. So God created man in his own image, in the image, of God He created him male: and female He created them. God blessed them and said to them, be fruitful and increase in number; fill the earth and subdue it. Rule over the fish of the sea and the birds of

Man has love but God is love.

the air and every living creature that moves on the ground. Then God said, I give you every seed-bearing plant on the face of the whole earth and every tree that has fruit with seed in it. They will be yours for food. And to all the creatures that move on the ground—everything that has the breath of life in it--- I give every green plant for food. And it was very good. And there was evening, and there was morning—the sixth day."

God took care to prepare everything we would need just as a Father provides for his children. He already knew the need of his children. In fact, God created all kinds of birds, animals, vegetation, fruits, trees, water, land, and more. Today, if a man takes time to prepare for himself and for his children, life will be far different for them. So many children in this world would not have to go through the terrible things they do. When you read the entire first chapter of Genesis you will come to understand how God started everything in the beginning so that He could have made things easy for His children. The fact is that God's perfect plan was to create humans with a mouth and belly. He created all kinds of fruits so man would have plenty to eat and be lacking in nothing. God made the whole land for man to live and to work it. The sea was made for man to fish and travel in. God's love cannot be explained. That is why we always say God is love, not God has love. Man has love but God is love.

You can have a good dad, a great step-father, the worst dad, average dad, inexperienced dad, you name it. Some people can say that they have a great father, so what do they need God for? God is the answer to everything. He is there no matter how good or bad things become. Earthly fathers can be great but they cannot put up with your mistakes. They run out of love or tolerate you up to a point. Sooner or later they may let you down, because it is written all humans will eventually go back to the dust from which they came. God is the only one that can comfort you when you are going through a deep situation. Sometimes not even a great father can help, only God can.

In fact, a true father is a man that is always in the presence of God. Meaning, to be in the presence of God is what connects you with Him. This enables you to act and function according to His divine nature. When this happens there is no way you can run out of love because if God truly dwells inside of you,

you will teach your children how
to put Him first.

Why the World Needs Godly Fathers

Be a friend

Be a dad

Be a man of God

Be a listener

And more

Being a religious father doesn't
mean you are a godly father.
Religious parents force their children to do things that fit the
particular doctrines of their religion. A godly father
understands his unperfected life in order to better understand
his children and he understands how to raise them in a godly
way. If you know how much God loves you and forgives you
over and over, and could grasp the plan He has for your life,
you will turn into a father that treats your children the way
you are being treated by God. This is the reason men need to
stay in the presence of God to accomplish the work of a father
toward their children.

8

WHAT ABOUT THE ABUSED CHILD?

As to a child that's been abused, what will be his future? A person that's been left out by a father needs to be very careful in life, why? Most of the people that do diabolical things against humanity are fatherless. Sometime they are acting this way because of hatred that's been swelling inside of them, sometimes for years. They project their anger against society. That's why it is hard for them to finish well in life or to become someone with value.

Some people have a desire to do something great but pride invades their mind causing them to only want to accomplish things to show people that they can put their father down as a way of revenge. When you do the same thing to the person who abused you, humiliated you, hated you, or abandoned you- that doesn't make you any better. In fact, it makes you worse than the person who made you miserable.

When God gives you the ability to change things around make sure you forgive and bring reconciliation.

When God gives you the ability to change things around, make sure you forgive and bring reconciliation to the person who hurt you so the name of Jesus can be lifted on high by everyone around you. Some fathers curse their children by saying things like, "You will never be anything. You will be a prostitute. No one is

85

going to love you," and so forth. In order to avoid these things from becoming your destiny, you have to implore these three things in your everyday life: discipline, obedience, and faithfulness. These are the three principles to follow in order to be blessed and be a blessing for others.

Discipline

Life without discipline can cause you to remain blind and believe that everything is ok when it is not. Eventually, you will have no way to get your life back in order to fix things. A lot of people suffer from a lack of discipline. Every day, throughout the world, people make easy and foolish decisions to allow things to go on without pressure. Stress sometimes helps you take control of your life better and causes you to be cautious, because after investing time, energy, and money in something, surely you will do whatever it takes to be successful. Discipline will take you far, as long as you don't give up. It takes discipline to get to your destiny. Being successful in school requires time, energy, and money. You may have to wake up early every day to be on time, even on days when you don't feel like going.

Discipline makes you set goals. It gives you power to put away unnecessary things in order to prioritize things that matter for your future. It helps you to do things that are not easy to do, especially if you are not used to prioritizing things that can cause you to get lazy. Some of those things are spending too much time on the Internet, being on Facebook, YouTube, and so on. Sometimes you may end up opening doors, watching porn and become addicted to it. It may be using your cell phone to text excessively or talking for hours, going to a party, spending a lot of time watching TV, and procrastinating when needing to do something valuable.

People that cannot discipline themselves will never be able to achieve great things in life. They will always be behind, even when they think they are moving forward. Without discipline the clock is moving, while leaving you behind.

Obedience

Romans 5:19 says, "For as by one man's disobedience many were made sinners, so by the obedience of one shall many be made righteous."

Redemption is necessary because of disobedience, which is at the center of man's problem. Redemption is God's solution. As we study the true meaning of obedience we will see the necessity of it for salvation, blessing and a God-honoring life.

Hebrews 11:8, says "By faith Abraham, when he was called to go out into a place which he should after receive for an inheritance, obeyed, and he went out, not knowing wither he went."

Abraham, like Noah, did not question the directive of God. This is a very important lesson here for all of us. Obedience is not based on understanding, but on faith in God and his wisdom.

Faithfulness

Faithfulness is having a true and constant support in keeping promises. As with all the fruits of the Spirit, God Himself is the model we must study for an example of faithfulness in order to be encouraged to turn and emulate Him. The faithfulness of God is a familiar phrase to those of a religious mind, but its' depth and scope are probably not as familiar. God's faithfulness seems to have been a favorite subject of Paul. He writes of it in first epistle (I Thessalonians) and again in what may have been his last (II Timothy). Paul had proved God in a thousand dangers and struggles. He found that when all was said and done that God had never failed him.

Other New Testament writers are equally expressive on this subject. Peter writes, "Therefore let those who suffer according to the will of God commit their souls to Him in doing well, as to a faithful creator" (I Peter 4:19). "Commit" is the word the Greeks would use when making a deposit with a trusted friend as we would do today to a bank. Christ committed His life to God all the way to the death, and we are to follow in His steps (I Peter 2:21). Paul responds with a similar statement in II Timothy 1:12, "For this reason I also suffer these things; nevertheless I am not ashamed, for I know whom I have believed and am persuaded that he is able to keep what I have committed to Him until that day."

Paul adds in II Timothy 2:13, "If we are faithless, he remains faithful; he cannot deny himself." When we speak of one another as being faithful, we mean that we adhere to our world, that we keep faith with men and discharge the obligation of our office or position. Because of these things we are trustworthy. It is much the same when we think and speak of God's faithfulness.

Usually, the first idea that comes to mind when God is called faithful is that He keeps His promises. Of course, this is included in the concept of God's faithfulness, but it interesting that it only appears twice in the New Testament. In Hebrews 10:23, Paul exhorts, "Let us hold fast the confession of our hope without wavering, for he who promised is faithful." Later, he writes that Sarah "judged him faithful who had promised" (Hebrews 11:11).

Paul's thought in II Timothy 2:13 goes far beyond even this. This verse tells us that we can trust in Him all the way to death because "he cannot deny himself." God's very nature and character constitutes a solemn obligation that He is bound by what He is and that He can never be, even in the smallest degree, contradictory or less than the level of his own consistent and uniform self. No wonder James 1:17 exclaims: "Every good gift and every perfect gift is from above, and comes down from the father of lights, with whom there is no variation or shadow of turning."

As God, He must be true to the character of goodness and wisdom that His very name implies. By contrast, a war goes on in us. Contradictory impulses and thoughts flood our minds. "For the flesh lusts against the spirit, and the spirit against the flesh" (Galatians 5:17) and we frequently lose the battle because the divine nature does not completely fill our minds. We blow hot and cold, dropping below our best selves.

No man is always who he truly is, but God is always Himself! As the Apostle John says, "God is light and in him is no darkness at all" (I John 1:5). There is nothing in God to mar his faithfulness in carrying out His word or His past acts. Our calling to Christ is one of God's past acts. This means that what God has begun in us He will complete all the way to salvation (Philippians 1:6). When we die, He will have prepared us for a responsibility in His family kingdom.

Struck in the performance of duty, faithfulness is the continuing of obedience; being true to one's word, promises, and vows. In other words, being steady in loyalty and remaining constant.

It takes great courage to remain faithful, especially with discipline and obedience, but there is a price to pay when you choose to walk in obedience. It's not about your wanting anymore; it's about what is required. If you are willing to be successful you have to follow all the requirements by setting up disciplines in your life that will eventually become your culture and will be the result of faithfulness.

9

THE EFFECTS OF AN ABSENT FATHER

An absentee father is one of the greatest failures on the face of the earth. He will tell others how many women he has slept with and how many children he has abandoned through abortions and rapes but he escapes personal responsibility for each one of them. Children may be abused because fathers are absent. Absentee fathers are doing a disservice to society. Their kids often struggle in the direction before them for lack of self-esteem or self-confidence.

> *An absentee father is the most failed person on the face of the earth.*

A father's love for his child should be unconditional. A father should be a best friend, someone you fear, not because he will harm you, but because you respect him. His purpose in life is to love you, to take care of you, to protect you and to guide you through your life decisions and support you in every aspect of your life.

My Story

Unfortunately, I am a fatherless child. I never had the opportunity to meet him. I was the first great-grandchild born in the family. Nevertheless, I was loved. My father's absence in my life was not felt as much as some because I had my uncle, who loved me and treated me like a princess. He would do anything for me, but he was not my father. I grew up calling someone else daddy all the time because I believed he was. He was not in my life as much because he was living in the United States.

I became a bit curious about him because he looked nothing like me, but bore a resemblance with other family members. I was about 10 years old when I began my quest to find out the truth about my real father. How can I call someone daddy who was my grandmother's sister's husband? It did not make sense. When I began to question my family members, one of my aunts made up a story about the man I was calling daddy. Immediately, I knew she was not telling the truth. No one in the family wanted me to know who he was. My little brain was still working, trying to figure it out. I decided to question my great-grandmother about him because I knew for sure she would not lie to me. So she said yes, you are right. The person you thought was your father is not. She described my father as this light-skinned, short young man who often came around the house to do some work. At the time I was asking her about him, she believed he was a bus driver, and that was all the information she shared.

You see, my mother gave birth to me at the very young age of 13. I am not sure how old my father was when I was conceived, which left me to question whether I was a child of a rapist. I can only assume since he was doing work in the house. It was a possibility he was a man, perhaps over 18, but the uncertainty is heart wrenching.

In Haiti, parents take their kids to school by means of bus, private cars, or private drivers. One morning, while I was waiting for the bus with my friend, I noticed the bus driver that stopped to pick us up resembled the person my great grandmother had described. He made my friend and I sit in the front seat without paying the bus fare. I could not believe it. All I could do was stare and wonder if this man was my father. On my way home from school, there he was again. He showed up and sat the two of us in the front seat again without paying the bus fare. When I got home I told my great grandmother what happened, and she said maybe it was your father. After that day, I never laid eyes on him again. What is the big secret I wonder? If my mother was raped, would it still be ok for me to want to know such an evil person? Why he did not try to find me? Did he love me? I wish all of these questions could be answered, but no one was communicating the truth, which led me to believe I was the child of a rapist. Even now, it is all a mystery.

I was six years old when a friend of the family started molesting me. I did not know what was going on, but for some odd reason I knew this was not supposed to happen. Of course, he told me not to say anything because it was our little secret, so I did not tell. He would show up in the house about twice a week and carry on the same wicked act. I wish I had the courage to make my uncle aware of what was going on, but I was only a child who thought if I told someone I would have gotten in trouble.

At the age of 11, I began to transition into my pre-teen years, showing signs of physical growth and development, which made me a target for another friend of the family to start molesting me. I could not believe that two different individuals were molesting me. Everyone in the family knew me to be a timid little girl that kept a lot to herself. Sometimes people thought I was a mean person, but it was the pain that I was suffering at the hands of these two molesters that made me appear indifferent. Even though the house was full of adults, they always found a way to bring me into a space where no one could see us and they would molest me. I did not understand what was going on. Was this normal? I was scared. I wanted someone to come and catch them in the act so the pain could stop, but no one ever did.

I often pondered if my biological father had been in my life would I have been subjected to such abuse? My father's protection was needed, but he was not there. He was nowhere to be found because I never met him. I endured this abuse for seven years, and my escape route was coming to the United States at the age of 13. I was finally free, so I buried that secret and never mentioned it.

I yearned for my father the most during my teenage years. I heard my peers talk about their dads, but I could not. My uncle was still a part of my life, but at times I still wanted to be daddy's little girl, especially when my mother punished me or when other people were being mean to me, calling me names. Words like "you are garbage" broke my heart.

Would my biological father ever call me such names? I just knew my father's presence in my life would have made a huge difference in my growing up. My freshman year in college, I decided it was time to try to locate my father, but all I had was a first name. When I asked my mother for a last name, she was not sure, so I put it to rest.

I heard a young woman in my presence say on time, "I love

you daddy" and something in me just died. I was broken inside. For the first time as an adult, I felt the true importance and meaning of a father because I never had the privilege to say utter those same words. Although I never met him, I think of him often because of all the pain I suffered when I was a child and all the mistakes I made in my relationships with men.

I had the love of my family, especially my uncle who spoiled me so much when I was a little girl. I did not let the absence of my father destroy me. I overcame the obstacles in my life and turned out to be the woman God intended for me to be. I have heard of many life events where children were molested and parents did not believe them. Parents, please listen to your kids and have an open mind. It does happen and is still happening. I did not have the courage of letting my family know what was going on because I was afraid of what they might think about me. Please pay attention to your children's behavior so you can help them before the abuse destroys them.

I share the pain of those with similar stories like mine. Words are truly powerful. It can make you or break you. I did not choose the negative words to break me, instead, I remain focused. Do not allow people's negative words to break you. Live for God, love God, worship God and He will take you to your point of destination.

10

A SELFISH FATHER

Selfishness by definition is when someone is concerned with one's self or primarily with one's own interest or benefits, regardless of the effect it may have on others. Selfishness makes man focus on what pleases him, even if others are going to suffer the consequences of his choices more than himself.

I went to evangelize with a group of people in prison. I asked one of the guys a question about his children. I said, "How would you protect your children if they chose not to go to school, or if they were hanging around with the wrong crowd?

I have seen so many men in the Pennsylvania upstate prison. They all mostly have children but they are blind with selfishness and pride.

Maybe they ended up prostituting themselves because of hunger? What if they are abused by their step-fathers, or when they become depressed they have no one to talk to? What happens when they are disrespecting their mothers, or when you are not there to love them? When they are scared of life, when they don't know who they really are, when they are in need for help, when they are feeling down, when they are confused about their choices in life, when they feel like they want to resign from going forward, when no one is there to encourage them, or when they are ready to kill themselves, what will you do?

Where are you in order to stop these things from happening to your children? Where are you when they are struggling because they feel they are not loved? Do you know who's hugging them when they need a father's hug?

I have seen so many men in the Pennsylvania upstate prison. Most men in prison have children, but are blinded with selfishness and pride. They have no idea what their loved ones are going through because of their absences. How can you stop these things from happening when they are going through all of these traumas? They are crying for your help, for your love and for your hugs, but you are not there.

Selfishness is when you don't know how to stay away from trouble that could result in prison time. It is when you use all manner of drugs that could destroy your brain. It is when you drink alcohol or smoke cigarettes that could result in liver damage, or worse. It is also when you keep sleeping with women all throughout the community, are addicted to porn, and masturbation, that could result in your getting a deadly sexual disease, and also when you are in the wrong business that could cause you to steal, kill and destroy someone else's life. That is selfish!

A woman cannot become pregnant without the seed of a man; therefore, you fathers play a big role in a beautiful creation God has made possible. So, why is it when women become pregnant with the most precious gift of all you abandon your responsibility as a father? The minute the child is conceived you are a father. It is imperative that you fathers begin planning for the future of your child. It is no longer about you, so stop being a narcissist. You must embody the qualities God instilled in you as a man. He will be pleased with your devotion for being good fathers. In Genesis 2:22 it states, "And the rib, which the Lord God had taken from man, made him a woman, and brought her unto the man." The challenging vocation of fatherhood can be astounding. The Scripture clearly makes us understand that women were made from man; therefore, all children come from you, man. Your presence in your child's life is a necessity, so please make them your priority.

Some of you men were raised in single mother households without ever seeing your father. I know it pains you greatly that your father was not present in your life, but his mistakes are not yours. Fathers, you are the sons of the Most High God. You cannot exert the limitations and inadequacies your father had to become him. Instead, do greater than he did. Do not let your father's mistakes define who you are or who you will become as a man. When fathers are involved in their children's lives, they make a great contribution in his or her future. If you are a constant presence in their lives, when life situations cause your paradigm to shift, you must believe the child will understand and try to work with you. He or she knows you have been the best provider you could be, and they will continue to be your greatest supporters.

So what is the reason for being a selfish father? To know the existence of your child and make a decision to be absent in their life is undeniably wrong. You have failed your children in everything. Children regard their fathers as their biggest role model. Instead of being there to embrace them and love them; some of you fathers chose to disappear.

The worst experience or memory a child has of their fathers are the constant broken promises. A father can be present in the home but still be selfish. A child wants to know their fathers will make them feel safe, and he is there for them. When a child says, my father is never there, it is time to take notice. On occasions, you can socialize with friends outside the home, but this should not be a daily routine. What about your children? You cannot regularly put your needs before your children. It is wrong. You should be thinking about investing your time with your children and the positive influence you need to be in their life. You are the protector and you have to guard them so they can be empowered by positivity and love.

Most fathers make time with friends they deem important, and in the process they forget about their most important assets, which are their sons and daughters. Fathers, your children grow up fast, do not resent them. Instead, try to become altruistic fathers and interact with them as it is very appreciated by them. Reflect on the times when you as a father have said you will be coming to visit them, and they look out the window and you never show up. That is the definition of a selfish father. You did not consider their feelings and the negative impact and affect the broken promises were going to have on their life. That was an act of selfishness and it can scar a child forever, or for a very longtime. Keep the promises you made to your children because it truly defines your character as a good man and a good father.

11

THE SILENT CHILD

When I remain silent because of all the hurts that are burning inside of me, no one really seems to understand even when they call me the quiet one.

Whenever they try to figure out the reason why I am so quiet they get me aggravated with the insults they use to try and figure me out. How are you going to be able to find out what is going on inside of me when you don't even know how to reach down to my level or walk in my shoes in order to speak my language or be willing to see things that have been hidden for years?

You may call me mean names, beat me up, talk about me behind my back, compare me with others, isolate yourself from me, use tricks that would aggravate me more or force me to do so. All these things cause me even more to bury myself into a deeper silence. Some people ask me why I keep everything inside, but they don't know what it's like when you watch your mom get a beating and abused almost every day by a violent father. I may hear my mom cry almost every night because she is being forced to have sex, even when she is sick. Do you know how many times I have been molested? Don't you know I have been put down every single day?

It's easy to use my silence against me by making fun of me, but you don't know my story. I hear your question! You ask me why I am cutting myself? Why am I depressed? Why am I suicidal? Why am I addicted with all kind of addictions?

You are using brutality to wake me up, but you fail to realize that it is this brutality that put me in that position, which is the reason my situation is very critical my friend. My crazy behavior turns you off completely. You think I don't know that? I do! The problem is that you are not helping me by looking down on me. Do you think I love the

I need your help that's why God let you see my problems not for you to talk about me.

situation that I am in right now, or do you think I planned to live this way forever? No! I need your help, that's why God let you see my problems, not for you to talk about me. Rather than talking about me, you have been given a great opportunity to help, so that I can get out of this miserable situation.

12

FOUR ANSWERS YOU NEED TO KNOW

Most young people spend their time complaining about what went wrong in the past. It is true that many fathers are messing things up, and they are responsible for what's going on in the prisons, in the streets, in homes, and in the clubs. Some people turn out to be real bad by doing dangerous things out there because they never received a fathers' love, but is recognition, in and of itself, going to change things? Complaining about the past helps you make excuses in order to make mistake after mistake and puts all the excuses for what happened on your father when you were a small kid. You can take pleasure in destroying yourself and excuse it by holding someone else responsible for it! The thing is, who's paying the price? That person

Will you be a child that is complaining for the past of your father as an excuse?

is already messed up, but if all you do in life is complain about that person's mess you will eventually turn out to be worse than they ever were.

Stop complaining or using someone else's mess as an excuse for your failures. Just move on in order to create a legacy in a positive way that will never be able to erased or destroyed.

How Can You Disconnect Yourself From The Curse of Your Father?

A Father's connection is always something that runs deep through the blood line. It is easy to become daddy-like when it comes to connecting through parental DNA.

The Bible teaches you what can happen when you don't know how to disassociate yourself from a negative heritage or from a generational curse. As an example, three generations repeated the same exact sin: Abraham, the father; Isaac, the son; and Jacob, the grandson.

"As Abraham was about to enter Egypt, he said to his wife Sarai, 'I know what a beautiful woman you are. When The Egyptians see you, they will say this is your wife. Then they will kill me but will let you live'" Genesis 12:11-12.

"When the men of the place asked about his wife, ISAAC said, 'She is my sister, for he was afraid to say, my wife, thinking the men of the place might kill me on account of Rebekah, for she is beautiful" Genesis 26:7.

"Leah, had a weak eyes, but Racheal was lovely in form, and beautiful. Jacob was in love with Rachel and said, I will work for you seven years in return for your younger daughter Rachel" Genesis 29:17-18.

All three generations had the same weakness. That's why they kept repeating the same sins from one generation to another. Therefore, you have to become spell breakers in order to disassociate yourself completely from such connections through your bloodline or genes. Pray the prayer in the chapter titled "Becoming a Curse Breaker."

Should You Finish Like Your Father?

The madness of not forgiving can cause you to finish worse than the person who did you wrong. Many people that have been abused many years ago never give themselves a chance to let go. They concentrate on thinking about what happened to them and as a result, they react bitterly with anger and resign from achieving great things in life. They hate their fathers and complain about what their fathers have done to them, but they're only causing more pain for themselves in the process. They possess the same character as their fathers by repeating the same mistake or even going beyond their father's sins which could cause them to finish just like their fathers. It is sad when we know something was wrong and how much it hurt us, and then end up doing the same thing or worse to our own children. This is what happens to many people. For this reason they can't finish well. Forgiveness is the weapon that could help people move forward. If they were to forgive, they would be able to focus on their goals in order to finish well and leave behind a legacy for their children.

How Can You Forgive Your Father?

After being abused or disappointed by a father it is hard to forgive that person. Especially when the person never apologizes verbally or in a written memo. it truly can make things impossible. A young lady I met in Canada said she was going through a lot. She was asking why God doesn't answer her prayers. One day, while I was praying for her I saw that she had been struggling with a situation between her dad and her, and I told her, she would have to deal with that situation first otherwise there will be no going forward. After giving her the message, she started crying and asked me, "How am I going to let him go after abusing me sexually?" I had to tell her, that's why you are so miserable and confused. The fact is that you don't know how to let him go. I spent some time that day ministering to her. She finally became convinced by the word and released her dad completely, thereby setting herself free. Weeks later, she received good news and everything worked on her behalf for the better.

Jesus forgave the whole world right at the cross while he had nails in his hands and feet, a crown of thorns, and blood dripping all over his body. People were making fun of Him but still Jesus said, "Father forgive them, for they know not what they are doing."

It is better to forgive someone instead of holding bitterness towards them in your heart because that can cause people to develop diseases that could lead to depression. Please forgive so that you can live the rest of your life free, with a good conscious and moving forward to achieve great things in life. Remember the Bible says: "Forgive and you will be forgiven."

13

BECOMING A CURSE BREAKER

Fathers can be under the spirit of Jezebel. Some fathers will leave the house at the drop of a hat or they have a house inside the house. They have lots of secrets and live under the influence of Beelzebub.

To become a spell breaker as a child of God, you must live in the presence of God. Some young people are fighting with spells in their life and demons have dominion over them.

If you don't break the curse, that curse is going to break you, eventually.

Michela had been molested many times. As a result, she started acting as a lesbian, sleeping with women and having sex with multiple men. She started taking and selling drugs, and dabbling in witchcraft. Her life was so complicated she wanted to kill herself by drinking a lot of alcohol because her life meant nothing to her.

If you follow the Bible closely you will see some sins are transferred through the bloodline up from a previous generation.

In order to break the spell or generational curse in your life, first you have to realize what kind of curses are running in the family and how it affects the people in your family because that same curse can affect you as well.

If you don't break the curse, that curse is eventually going to break you. When you are under a curse that takes control of your life you can do things that can destroy your destiny. If you realize that you are under an influence that makes you do things in a strange way, the deliverance prayer is for you and you will never be the same in the name of Jesus. The beauty of women caused untold generations of men from Abraham to David to be affected and so on.

In Genesis 12:10-16 it reads, "Now there was a famine in the land; so Abraham went down to Egypt to sojourn there, for the famine was severe in the land. It came about when he came near to Egypt, that he said to Sarai his wife, see now, I know that you are a beautiful woman; and when the Egyptians see you, they will say, this is his wife; and they will kill me, but they will let you live. Please say that you are my sister so that it may go well with me because of you and that I may live on account of you. It came about when Abraham came into Egypt, the Egyptians saw that the woman was very beautiful. Pharaoh's officials saw her and praised her to Pharaoh; and the woman was taken into Pharaoh's house. Therefore he treated Abraham well for her sake; and gave him sheep and oxen and donkeys and males and females servants and female's donkeys and camels."

Abraham sinned against God twice by lying and saying that Sarai wasn't his wife). Isaac repeated the same sin as his father Abraham.

Genesis 26:6-7, "So Isaac stayed in Gerar. When the men of that place asked him about his wife and he said, "She is my sister." Because he was afraid to say, "She is my wife." He thought, "The men of this place might kill me on account of Rebekah, because she is beautiful."

Jacob despised Leah because of the beauty of Rachel.

Genesis 29:15-20, "Laban said to him, Just because you are a relative of mine, should you work for me for nothing? Tell me what your wage should be. Now Laban had two daughters; the name of the older was Leah and the name of the youngest one was Racheal. Leah had weak eyes, but Rachel had a lovely figure and was beautiful. Jacob was in love with Rachel and said, "I will work for you seven years in return for your younger daughter Rachel." Laban said, "It's better that I give her to you than to some other man. Stay here with me." So Jacob served seven years to get Rachel, but they seemed like only a few days to him because of his love for her."

The same sin reached down through the years and affected David and his son Ammon.

2 Samuel 11:1-2, "In the spring, at the time when kings go off to war, David sent Joab out with the king's men and the whole Israelite army. They destroyed the Ammonites and besieged Rabbah. But David remained in Jerusalem. One evening David got up from his bed and walked around on the roof the palace. From the roof he saw a women bathing. The women was very beautiful."

Generational curses are so complicated to understand, even when people see it destroying one another in the family. Many times no one wants to take a stand and say something.

Prayer That Leads To Salvation

If you don't know Jesus as your personal Savior will you repeat this simple prayer?

"Lord Jesus, I believed you are the son of God who died for my sins and resurrected three days after, and You are now sitting at the right of the Father in heaven. Please be my Savior by converting my life. I believe I am saved in Jesus' name."

After reciting this prayer you feel free to contact us for more help.

Prayer that Breaks Spells in 21 Days or Less

"God is our refuge and strength,
And ever-present help in trouble.
Therefore we will not fear, though the earth give way
And the mountains fall into the heart of the sea,
Though its waters roar and foam
And the mountains quakes with the surging.
There is a river whose streams make glad the city of God,
The holy place where the most high dwells.
God is within her, she will not fall;
God will help her at break of day.
Nations are in uproar, kingdoms fall;
He lifts his voice, the earth melts.

The lord Almighty is with us;
The God of Jacob is our fortress.
The desolations he has brought on the earth.
He makes wars cease
To the end of the earth.
He breaks the bow and shatters the spear;
He burns the shields with fire.
He says, "Be still, and know that I am God;
I will be exalted among the nations,
I will be exalted in the earth.
The Lord Almighty is with us;
The God of Jacob is our fortress."
-Psalm 46

The Warfare Prayer

"I rebuke every curse in my life. Curses from my parent's generation. Curses that follow me every step I take and curses that are blocking me from walking in progress to get to my destiny. No Spirits of abuse, spirits of molestation, nor the spirit of humiliation can kill, destroy or steal my dreams. I declare and I decree no weapon formed against me shall prosper!

The blood of Jesus covers me against any covenant made in the past and every covenant that my parents or grandparents made by using my name, in the name of Jesus. I am free from all curses that were following me."

ABOUT THE AUTHOR

Dr. Ansy and his wife are the founders of Ansy Dessources Ministries and the senior pastors over Healing Center Community Church based in Levittown, Pennsylvania. Dr. Ansy was raised in Haiti and moved to the United States in the late 1990s. Dr. Ansy received the call on his life at a very young age, and began walking out his calling at the age of 21.

He is a cutting-edge, energetic speaker that has a passion to aggressively fulfill the Great Commission that Christ gave to His disciples to go into the world and make disciples of all people. He has a heart for those who do not know Jesus. His giftings are evident by his fruit. He is anointed through the Holy Spirit and this is evident through miracles, prophetic gifting, and the power of God being shown through his worship and preaching. He is a voice that God is using to break the chains that are binding people today and teaching them to declare the freedom that is a gift offered to those who call Jesus Christ their Lord and Savior.

He has ministered in different countries and is a voice God is using to reach people, not only in America, but all over the world. Dr. Ansy Dessources is also the author of *Destiny- A Living Miracle.*

Dr. Ansy Dessources

Made in the USA
Las Vegas, NV
05 January 2022

40446534R00069